i

GEOMETRON

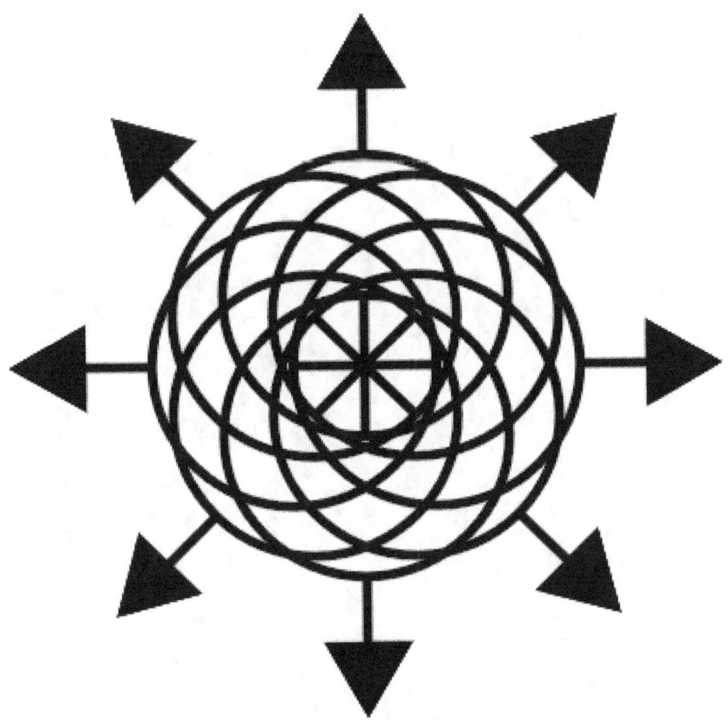

MAGIC

by Trash Robot

Geometron Magic

Trash Robot

January 20, 2022

Contents

List of Figures

Chapter 1

Magic

Our aim is to share technology which makes all of the elements of a good life free for all people everywhere. The technology we need to do this exists. From cheap local renewable energy to dense growth of food to safe disposal of waste, we have all the material elements of a life of plenty created by our shared knowledge. And yet we live lives constantly hounded by scarcity based on activities which are in the process of killing us all. Why? What is missing from our collective lives? This work is an attempt to answer these questions and to provide a path forward using new ways of engaging with existing technology to build the social structures needed to get from a path of destruction and scarcity to one of creation and plenty.

Our current model of how we think of technology and

"the economy" is based on production and consumption. In the modern world, material is extracted from the Earth, is processed into "products", which eventually turn into waste, and then the process repeats. This process will always produce scarcity, as everyone must compete for the limited resources. That scarcity is managed by people claiming ownership over the land from which resources are extracted, ownership of the machines which produce products, and control of the workers making the things.

We cannot continue with this model because in a finite world it will always consume all resources and destroy all life. We should not continue because it inflicts misery and fear on all but the small group of people who own and/or control the system.

Furthermore, even things which are not based on this model, like writing books or software which can freely replicate on existing hardware, are forced to conform to the basic logic of this model. While money no longer literally represents metal dug up from the ground, the *metaphor* of money is still based on that. No matter what anyone does, we all need money in our existing system to survive. Under the existing system if a group of people with no money all want to build a thing, they can't do it without someone with money-creation authority blessing the activity. People can physically do it in theory, but as long as the material needs of survival are controlled by people who demand money for those things no one but the rich can afford the luxury of doing useful things for which there is no monetary incentive. This means that the more people in society produce things which *don't* require digging things up or doing manual labor, the larger the gap will be between the money production process and actual creation of value. This is the reason inequality will always get worse as the information economy grows. Everyone in the information economy is making money from replication, while the old economy still runs on production. The more powerful information technology becomes, the larger this gap will become, and the rate of increase will keep accelerating.

What we need to recognize in order to move beyond this system is that we must transition from a consumer society to a replication society, and to change our value system to reflect that. In the last 300 years we have dug up a staggering quantity and diversity of material. None of what we have dug up to build our shared global industrial civilization in the last few centuries is really "thrown away". It's all still here, and generally way more of it than we want. Some of it is in landfills, some of it is in wasteful machines that have no reason to exist other than to keep "the economy" going, and some of it is in poisoned water and soil, but all of it is still around us in some way.

The laws of physics and chemistry will allow us to re-use all these elements indefinitely just as natural ecosystems have with simpler elements for the duration of life on Earth. We can in some sense think of all the trash, toxic waste and useless junk we have created as the "hardware" on which we want to create the "software" of a just and sustainable future. In this model, value comes from the power of replication, rather than production.

In a consumer society, every producer is in competition with every other producer. In a replication society, creators benefit from replication. This creates an incentive system for creators which is the opposite of the existing one. If I find a way to extract a poison from a river using simple and readily available materials and transform it into a usable material for building things, it is in my best interest for that to replicate. I want other people to copy it because only then will *all* the water get cleaned up. I want other people to copy it because the more people copy it the more people will improve upon it, and I will end up with a vastly superior technology to the one I started with, making the river I live on cleaner than would have been possible without the broader community of creators.

Replication societies are nothing new. They are much older than the production model. Any indigenous society which lives in equilibrium with its environment is replication based. When people living in a forest use a tree to make a boat to hunt an animal, that is a replication economy. They use culture to replicate the boat-making process, and stewardship of the forest to make sure there are always more trees and animals. The old boats rot and turn into soil which gets turned back into trees, they teach their children to pass along the system after they die and turn back into soil themselves, and the system replicates. What we propose here is to take this older and proven social model used by indigenous civilizations and apply it to the materials and principles of modern machines.

So how do we do this? If all the science needed to build a replication based civilization exists, why are we not doing it now? To build this world we must recognize what the hard part is about this. It's not building the things, we know how to do that. It's not organizing people to do things, we also know how to do that. It's the replication of the *desire* to replicate a thing. That is what we call "magic" for the purpose of this work. We use this term because no other term fully expresses the mystery of the process by which we acquire the desire to do a thing.

Under the current system, desire to replicate plays a minimal or hidden role. Most people work for money out of fear, create the systems to do that out of greed, and consume based on being controlled by a media which exists for the sole purpose of stimulating consumption. All these processes are separated from one another. We produce at a "job" and consume separately. Anyone not producing or consuming using money is treated as a burden on the system.

But if we want technology to replicate freely, we need

to harness that spark which causes a person to suddenly feel a desire to create and share a new thing. That spark cannot be reduced to rules and numbers and laws of physics. It is the spark that makes us human, which gives us free will or the human spirit or soul.

Every single technology we use today relies on this magic. Every computer, every jet airplane, every factory and medicine–all these things began with some spark in an actual human which was passed on to other humans. Technology producers today have mechanistic models for their technology which ignore life. We use the provocative term "magic" to re-center all our thoughts about technology on life itself, starting with the human spirit and going out to the living world around us. Life is self-replicating and we identify this word "magic" with all living things. We reject any model for our world which is not centered on the magic of life itself.

So where does this leave us? We want to transition back to a replication society while retaining the most useful modern technologies. We are currently trapped in a system based on scarcity that no one can leave. So how do we get from one to the other? We must first recognize that the most powerful engine of change in modern society is social networking. Working alone, any technology we create is of almost no use. Everything we create requires that we find ways to collaborate and find people to share with. The core technology which structures all other technology is how we communicate with one another in complex networks. If we want to build a radically different world, we must therefore build a radically different social network. This work represents the creation of a social network for the sole purpose of empowering this replication economy.

The transition from a consumer to replication society means replacing the "means of production" with the "means of replication" as the fundamental element of our model of society. Of course we will still have machines that build more machines and people operating those machines just as we do today. But we recognize that the most fundamental thing is not those machines but the social network which tells others how to build those machines and more importantly *why* they should build those machines. This transmission of the "why" is what makes the process require our use of the term "magic".

In order for this to work we need to have media which supports self-replicating documents which tell us how to replicate technology, and this media itself must be self-replicating. This means the media must carry on it documents which in addition to copying freely from one device to the next must tell people how to copy the actual physical devices.

Once this process gains momentum we can use it as the basis of a whole new economy which allows us to progress into a full replication system. However, initially we are back to the problem of trying to survive without money in a system which literally won't let us live without it. Our way out of this is with a middle path in which we build social media on hardware which can be bought cheaply and given away to the community as a free resource for very little money and with no material input from any central entity like a company. In order for this to scale, each time someone copies the system it must provide more value added up in monetary units than it costs to build the copy, including the labor to put it together.

This is much easier than it sounds. Social media today is a centralized form of power which generates trillions of dollars in commerce, all based on software. That software has its replication deliberately crippled by intellectual property so that a very small group of digital landlords can take money from everyone else in the system. They get away with this because of the very real value created by linking us all up with one another in complex ways. From ride sharing to finding friends to selling and buying things, all commerce can be dramatically enhanced by social networking. If it costs under 1000 dollars to build out a local social network of free book-like documents for a community, all we need is for that to provide 1000 dollars of value and it will replicate. In even a small and poor community this is an infinitesimal fraction of the available commerce which can be amplified by social media.

We do not aim to build a "new social media platform". We aim to build hundreds of millions of truly independent social media platforms, all of which simply replicate documents from one to another, and all of which exist for the primary purpose of building out the replication economy which will transition us off of consumption.

To do this in the long run we will rebuild the hardware from the ground up along the principles of Geometron laid out here. But we can't get there until we have a network which is financially self-sustaining in the existing system. At its core this means finding a way to harness the "magic", the core spark which makes a person want to engage with a thing.

Geometron is a way of thinking about technology in which we think of all technology as a geometric construction. Shaping metal into machines is a geometric construction. Displaying symbols on a screen or on paper is a geometric construction. Printing electronic circuits on a board or chip is a geometric construction. All the symbols we use to communicate with one another are geometric constructions. In Geometron we rethink how we program and control machines based on this idea that geometric constructions are more fundamental than those using numbers. Numbers are useful tools, but we choose as a matter of values to always place them in a subordinate role to geometry.

This is the origin of the term "Geometron": "geometry" combined with the "-tron" ending which is associated with machines. The work here demonstrates using this method of geometric programming to create a wide variety of useful things. We replace "computer programs" made up of numbers, algebra and broken English with geometric constructions represented with geometric symbols.

This book is therefore combining "Geometron" with "magic" by building social media based on these ideas about self-replicating media and geometric thinking, together in a combined whole. The previous book of Geometron was more technical and also less action oriented. This work intends to both tell you why we need to build this system and very specifically how you can immediately engage by copying parts of it and recruiting other people to copy more of it. We are asking readers to *participate* actively through direct action. We are asking you to tell people about this, to share these ideas and build on them. We are asking you to help us build a world of abundance from the bottom up through direction action.

Finally, we must address the problematic connotations of the word "magic" and why we choose to use it anyway. Many people of many religious beliefs either view "magic" as a word referring to the "superstition" of other people's beliefs or some literal power in the physical world outside of the realm of science. In this work we are using the word to refer to an observable phenomenon in the world which everyone agrees happens, and which applies to everyone's religious, spiritual, or philosophical beliefs. Every belief, be it one called "religion", "philosophy", "ideology", or "science", is based on this replication from person to person. Beliefs are held by mortal people. We all die. Our minds decay. We forget. What brings beliefs of *all* kinds to life is their replication. And this is never just the mechanical process of printing or broadcasting media or preaching in person. It is the process that happens deep inside us in which each of us shifts our internal reality, our internal *desires* in a way which accommodates the new belief system. This can and does happen with everything we believe. While one person might not believe in the god of another, none of us should deny the basic observable phenomenon by which the other person's belief replicated to get to the point that they believed it. We can call that replication a "magic" without attributing to it any supernatural connotation.

We hope that people of all faiths can use this framework in a productive way to build new ways of life. Geometron and Trash Magic are not religious systems. They are systems of organizing information and materials which can be fit into any existing religion. In order for this movement to work we must find ways to be compatible with all existing faiths, and not to attempt to convert to some new faith. Just as we find all faiths using oil and mine based supply chains today, and communicating their faiths via the Internet, we will build a world where all those people are able to carry on their lives in a post-extraction framework without creating contradictions with the other parts of their cosmology separate from the mines and pipelines we seek to replace. This does not make Geometron and Trash Magic "non religious" or "religious", but occupying a different space in the human mind and experience and being boosted by the replication of what is already being replicated. We must therefore build many "magics" which are compatible with all existing human belief systems, and which can replicate along with them in their institutions.

Chapter 2

Trash Magic

Trash Magic is a mode of existence in which we can replicate everything we need to live a good life locally using the waste streams of the existing consumer system. We are using the word "magic" as in the rest of this work to refer to the replication of the desire to replicate things made from trash.

Full Trash Magic is the ultimate objective of all this work. Under full trash magic, all people, everywhere in the world, can get food, shelter, medicine, media, sanitation, water, heating and cooling, and the machines to produce all these for free locally. We will abolish all mining, all oil and gas extraction and all global physical supply chains.

In order to achieve this objective we begin small, with something that immediately provides value, and scale up based on replication of the thing which provides value. If we can do even the simplest thing which just barely provides a small amount of value from trash but *replicates* and *evolves* with intent, we can then simply guide that evolution and growth to navigate to the complete system as we engage more and more people with more and more specialized skills and resources.

To start all this, we turn to the industrial revolution as a guide. Much of what powered the industrial revolution was using new energy sources in the form of coal and steam to build machines which build other machines. Also, textiles have always played a central role in technology replication, as their products become central to people's culture, which replicates and brings the textile production machines along with them.

In analogy to all this, we want to build the smallest possible factory, which we call a Trash Factory, which mimics this pattern but without mining. We want to build machines that can build machines, or a machine shop, powered by the local forces of the Sun, wind, and flowing water. A machine shop is a collection of tools which can work metal into the forms needed to make more machines. Machine shops are how metal machines traditionally replicate themselves. We need to be able to melt metal waste into metal ingots then process that into bars, sheets, rods, wires and blocks. Then we need milling machines, lathes and drill presses to machine them into desired shapes. We need the tools of sheet metal work like the brake and bender. We need an arc welder, torches and some other basic tools for soldering, welding and brazing. All this must be made from trash.

Building a machine shop can be based to a large extent on junk cars. Cars have plenty of steel, plenty of parts to salvage without any melting or casting, and electrical tools which can be used for motors and so on. As much as possible we will use things as we find them without reprocessing. If we can, we'll just get donated old stuff that is broken and fix it. The machine shop maintained by people good at fixing broken stuff is as old as the industrial revolution, we just aim to build this into the rest of our self-replicating media system.

The machine shop also needs to have tools for working plastics, with molding on metal molds created using the metal shop, and plastic welding and rework tools. An electrical shop is needed for electric motors and generators.

A fully functioning machine shop which is optimized to build more machines from junk cars can be a self-replicating and self-sustaining factory just by selling machines. We can sell drill presses, milling machines and the like for money which can support the people who build and maintain the system.

In addition to the machines which replicate themselves, we will build all the tools for creating trash-based clothes on site. We will build or fix broken sewing machines, and use them to create fashionable and functional original clothing of all kids for all people for free to those in the most need. If our story replicates as we hope it does, and people believe in our mission, we should be able to support all the work to build the system, to operate it, and to deliver the free clothes to those in need by selling high end fashion to those who can afford it. All clothes are made on site with waste clothing donated from those in physical proximity to the Trash Factory.

All the motive power for Trash Factories is provided by one of three main sources: heat engines, water drive, and wind. An essential technology which must be integrated into the first generation of Trash Factory is the trash-built Stirling Engine. This is a very simple heat engine developed in the 1800s and used widely ever since which can turn heat into mechanical motion by compressing and decompressing a gas in a sealed chamber with a piston. These engines have been overshadowed by the internal combustion engine or the giant steam turbines used in large scale commercial power plants, but they work well and are well understood and simple. The primary means of driving a heat engine in Trash Magic(without setting things on fire) is using the energy of the sun focused via mirrors onto a heat absorber. Large arrays of mirrors can be built from trash which track the sun and maintain the focus of the sun over a large area onto the absorber. The other robotics technology that is part of Geometron can be used to steer the mirrors as the angle of the sun changes. Stirling engines can also be run backwards, creating a heat pump when the shaft is turned. This means they can be used to cool things, being the basis of solar-powered air conditioning and solar-powered refrigeration. Solar powered air conditioners sound almost too good to be true, but this has been demonstrated well over 100 years ago, it is just not used today for economic and social reasons. The heat engines are also a very good commercial product which can be sold(as an off-grid power source) for money to support the rest of Factory operations.

Water and wind are both pretty traditional: we simply build rotors for both from trash and source the drive trains and generators from trash. Water can be waves, tide or streams/rivers/creeks. In all cases, we envision a factory which has between 1 and 5 people operating it at a time using between 1 kW and 100 kW.

The absolute maximum available solar power in direct sunlight on a clear day is about 1 kW per square meter so at 100% efficiency(which will never happen) this is up to about a 100 square meters. If we imagine getting a pessimistic 10% efficiency, that's up to 1000 square meters, which is about 30 meters on a side or about 100 feet on a side square(about a quarter acre or 0.1 hectares).

A reasonable site for a Trash Factory will be about 1 acre, or about 4000 square meters or 0.4 hectares. This will be enough space for a machine shop, the power station, and the various staging areas we need for incoming waste streams and outgoing product streams. When possible we site near flowing natural water and use extra power to both pump water uphill and to clean it up for drinking. Water can then be both used to drink and used to get energy back out as it flows downhill from a water tower or hill top reservoir. Our goal is to be a very scaled-down version of the River Rouge factory from the Ford Motor Company from the early 20th century, where a constant flow of raw trash(instead of raw material from a mine) comes in one side and a flow of finished manufactured goods flows out the other side.

The Trash Factory can be sited based on convenience to resources, cheap land zoned for heavy industrial activity, and easy access. It does not have to be an ideal retail location. The retail side of the Trash Factory is free stores and existing shops. We can make things to directly provide for free for those who want, providing warmth and protection with fashionable and well-fit clothes sourced from local trash while also sourcing products for local stores shelves we sell for money to support the Factory. This also applies to all the machines produced in the machine shop: we can sell welders at a welding shop, heat pumps through an HVAC(heating, ventilation, and air conditioning) distributor, drill presses and machine tools to auto shops, etc. Also, providing a mix of free and commercial products to our local community creates the human relationships we need to establish to keep our supply chain flowing of trash we get for free from existing waste streams.

Again, the Trash Factory aims to always produce more value than it consumes, both bringing in enough cash to support the people operating it and the land and also providing material support for whoever is the most wanting in the local community. Every kilogram of mass we convert from trash to products locally takes that kilogram of mass out of both the landfill waste stream and the mine stream of consumer society. If we can make this replicate and evolve, we can keep removing more and more energy from that system over time, and pumping more and more energy into our system. As long as replication of this system takes less energy than replicating the existing systems we will naturally consume the old system for reasons of simple thermodynamics.

But where does "Trash Magic" fit in with all this? Trash Magic refers to the transmission of this system of trash-built and trash-sourced factory using the self-replicating media platform described in this work. Every machine, article of clothing, every clever hack and structure of business or organization will be documented in a library of books(including this one) which are kept on free media and network infrastructure we build into all of our systems. In the beginning this will be the Raspberry Pi(a very cheap and open source computer) based system which starts building our network, along with off the shelf commercial wireless network infrastructure. As we develop our system it will evolve into the fully trash-built media described later in this work.

Full Trash Magic involves taking the Trash Factory system described here and scaling it up to all things we need. As we grow we always direct all excess value created by the system into helping the most needy in the immediate physical community around the Factory. As this pulls more energy into the system, we will be able to get access to more land and resources outside the property system. Directing resources to those with the most needs first will abolish poverty in very localized areas. Abolition of local poverty will enable more space outside of the property system to flourish, on which we can create products which are all outside the property system.

This will ultimately include the whole set. We need to build fresh water generators from dirty water, and build a toilet infrastructure which turns human waste into compost which is used to grow things locally including organic fiber crops for toilet paper(which can also be a product of the Factory). This waste disposal and composting system will be integrated into a system of local synthetic biology, where we use modern biotechnology techniques to control microorganisms and fungi to make all the medicine we need on site. Again, building bioreactors which can make all medicine is nothing new, we just need enough human energy in the system that we can attract the talent in the form of experts who already know how to build such systems. Our aim initially is not to invent anything, but to create the social connections which allow people with expertise to connect with real local community needs and then to scale that through self-replicating media. If we can make clean water, machines, clothes, medicine, food, and media on site, we have a system which can sustain human life without mining or oil as is our goal. You can think of our whole social media system as like a ride share app but for finding the people with whom we build a sustainable civilization.

Again, we must reiterate that this is not some futuristic hypothetical technology. Creating free web pages on free computers which tell you how to make things from trash is simple. Making things from trash is known. The waste is plentiful. 300 years of industrial production brings the whole periodic table of elements right to your doorstep. The needs of the most impoverished and marginalized people in any given local community are known. The mass peer-to-peer media network of the Internet exists which can spread all of this. All we are saying with this work is that these dots can be connected. The only thing missing is the *will* to connect these dots. And of course while we might already have the will to do it, what we need to make it scale is the ability to create specific detailed plans and replicate the desire to carry those out. The media platform documented in the rest of this work will allow us to do this. The revenue we will generate by simply building the free social network of free books will provide the startup capital(not financial capital, but resources like land and human attention) to build our first Factories.

Full Trash Magic can exist on just a few acres with just a few dozen people. We can achieve this in our lifetimes if we focus on our objective and work together!

Chapter 3

The Pibrary

The Pibrary is a network of free books distributed using the Raspberry Pi, a very cheap open source computer designed primarily for educational use. The goal of the Pibrary is to be an extension of the public library system into more public spaces and with more free and more local books.

The Pibrary represents a fully free network, meaning everything is free of copyrights or other intellectual property, everything is available in a public space for use by whoever wants to use it, and everything can be freely replicated by other people in other places.

The Pibrary is centered on public spaces, meaning spaces anyone can get access to without any restrictions such as public parks or public streets or any other outdoor space which we do not restrict access to based on money. This can include private property as long as the owners of the property are willing to create a truly open space which welcomes all people regardless of social or economic status on a 24/7 basis.

The free computing element of the Pibrary consists of mobile Raspberry Pi computers with portable battery and solar panel as a free community computing resource for use in public spaces by whoever has the greatest need for free access to information. This can be an extension of other mutual aid projects like Food Not Bombs which provide basic goods and services for free to the most marginalized people in public spaces. The solar panels and batteries can be used to power or charge mobile devices, a critical infrastructure need for unhoused or traveling people. The Raspberry Pis are installed with no private data, no logins, no passwords, and are intended to be used that way so that they can be safely shared. The only purpose of the Pi is to access the Internet for free, just like a free public computer in a public library.

The basic Raspberry Pi mobile terminal setup consists of the Pi board which is about the size of a deck of cards and costs about \$60, the SD card the operating system is installed on, a keyboard, a mouse, a small mobile screen, a 12 volt lead acid battery, and a solar panel and charger. The whole system costs about \$400 and can all be purchased online from many vendors. In order to charge devices the kit must also have a 12 volt USB power hub to break out the battery power for charging

USB devices.

The Raspberry Pi is also used as a home web server for creating, editing and sharing the self-replicating documents of the Geometron system. To run a Pi at home we need a lot less infrastructure. The keyboard and mouse and a standard TV or computer screen can be used once to set it up, it can be powered off of a wall plug, and then run "headless" with no screen or peripherals, accessed over entirely over the network. This server can be accessed by people anywhere in the world by using port forwarding over the home router or router in a public space to connect it to the outside Internet.

Internet access is provided for free in public spaces by wireless hotspots with clearly posted log on information. We can beam Internet into public spaces with directional antennas and wireless network extenders. All of this physical infrastructure is provided for free by donors from the local community. It is a public resource.

The primary purpose of all the media hosted on the Pibrary system is to create a free library of books which contain all the knowledge required to build a society based on the principles of the last chapter: built from trash and powered from the sun, wind and water. This will include science, technology, history, culture, commerce, and any other deep knowledge about and for a local community. All of these books consist of collections of documents which replicate freely from one server to another without any restrictions. Each copy of each book can also be edited, deleted, or moved around on any server by anyone at any time.

We must emphasize that we did not invent building useful things from trash and using them to help people. What we are doing is gathering and curating a collection focused on this. We are creating a layer of knowledge which is more focused than a search engine or wiki, which is exactly as broad a range of knowledge as we need to do our work to build a better world locally in a specific space and no more. We are not replacing the Internet, the public library, or Wikipedia, we are creating a new layer of curated and focused knowledge on top of these.

The Pibrary is a network of free self-replicating books. This is not a network of users. There is no private data, there are no users, no logins, no passwords, no encryption, and no databases. While we are creating a vast universe of documents, each Pibrary will have a collection which is limited based on a focus of immediate interest for a relatively small community with a shared purpose. Initially this just means the books created by Trash Robot to share the ideas of this network itself.

Part of the infrastructure of the Pibrary is domain names for public use which can host copies of all the documents in our system. All of these public web pages, like the Raspberry Pi servers, have no private data, no users, and no databases. Anyone can copy files onto them and off of them, or delete them at will. Pages can be forked down to make more libraries with more books and more libraries inside libraries. Whole forks can be deleted by anyone at any time. Our resilience against deleting is to constantly copy books to many places again and again. We are building media which behaves as a living organism, replicating, dying, and evolving as part of our culture as humans.

The domain names for these public web pages are selected to correspond to public spaces like streets, parks or bodies of water, with top level domains other than .com so that they are not commercial and not personal. Some volunteer from the community can buy the domain and pay for commercial cloud hosting at some standard web hosting vendor, and install the system on that server. It generally costs about 10 dollars a year for the domain registration and another 10 dollars a month or so for the hosting. As long as our network is providing significant community benefit this should be a relatively minor cost to get paid for by a volunteer.

We create physical flags to display in public spaces which point to the domains which host the books. These flags are created by sewing solid rainbow colored felt letters in a block font onto a black cloth background about 3 feet by 3 feet square. Flags, like everything else, are meant to be copied widely and displayed publicly. Flags fly in physical spaces which are represented by domains which host books we create, edit and replicate using the network of free Raspberry Pi computers.

Another powerful tool in our network of self-replicating

books is Github. Github is a company which provides
free(free for open source and that includes everything we
do) hosting of documents which can be copied from anywhere on the Web. We can create private instances of
Geometron servers on home personal computers which
have local web servers set up which only run on that machine. These are used to edit local copies of the whole
system including any books we want to save. As these are
replicated and edited, they can be "pushed" to Github
with Github Desktop, a GUI(graphical user interface)
app. Using Github to move books around provides a
backup where if servers are all wiped out the data can't be
edited without access to a personal Github account which
is based on Github's security. Also Github has enough
bandwidth and protection against surges in bandwidth
that it can be a source for replication to many servers all
at once. Anyone anywhere in the world can copy whole
libraries of books with simple clicks in their web browser
to their personal Github repositories, then push it out to
the public and copy from there to any other server. This
network of potentially millions of Github accounts and
millions of Raspberry Pi's and millions of domain names
can be constantly supporting a free flow of replication of
books from server to server across the globe.

The format of "books" on the Pibrary is the "magic
book" described in the next chapter. This library of
free books can form the basis of a social network which
provides the same benefits as modern networking appli-

cations but with direct community control. Books can be created to document all commerce, organized by the people engaging in that commerce. The same efficiency improvements which are currently monetized by Silicon Valley can then be kept in local communities, which will bring in enough wealth to materially support the people building the network. As the amount of wealth generated by the network increases we will direct all excess to those in the local community with the most need.

The use of the Network to direct resources to those in the most need is mutual aid. The network helps people and those people help the network by representing it in public, sharing the information with as many people as possible. This applies to everyone. As the network generates more wealth it should be possible to eliminate poverty in very localized areas covered by the network. As this happens we can use the network to build more and more industries up using the Trash Factories and this can amplify the process. Network value in commercial activity funds industrial value which funds more network expansion and so on. As the network grows and we can support more people, those people can solve harder and harder problems and scale up what we can make in the Trash Factories more and more. As this knowledge is generated, it will all be synthesized into more free self-replicating books which are published onto the Pibrary network. So our manufacturing supports growth of the network, but the network is also supporting the growth of manufacturing by replicating all the knowledge required to copy our processes.

The Pibrary creates and enhances public spaces. Selecting the right physical space to inhabit for this is one of the most important parts of building a successful network. We need to choose spaces that have the absolute maximum possible intersection of people. We must ask the question: if a place is about 10 yards across, what place in a given area a couple miles across has the widest range of people crossing it in any given day? Of places like this, what is the most freely accessible? We must evaluate accessibility based on sidewalks, access by car, access by public transit, by bike, wheelchair, or any other means of access relevant to the local community. But we must also consider accessibility in terms of it being legal to be there, there being adequate restroom facilities nearby, places to rest or work or sleep, shade or other shelter, and a generally welcoming culture.

The public space being activated by a Pibrary does not need to always have a Raspberry Pi or solar panel. It can just have a flag or sign or markers which point to the domain which has the copies of the books maintained about that place. It can even be invisible, with a known domain being used by people about a place without any obvious infrastructure in that place other than the place itself.

The Raspberry Pi can also serve as a monitor for the environment, measuring aspects of the water, air, soil, living things and anything else of interest to the community. In rural areas, sequences of wireless network repeaters on off-grid power can go along rivers and streams with local Raspberry Pi's with sensors measuring water properties and delivering that information via the web to the rest of the network. This can put the land, life, and water itself onto the network and connect all of us humans on the network more intimately with these systems.

Chapter 4

The Magic Books

The media which drives this network is the Magic Book. The Magic Book is a format for electronic books which lends itself to easy replication across the Internet and easy editing. We use the term "magic" as in all other places in this work to mean that people replicate them themselves. That is, with simply copy/pasting links and clicking on them in browsers anyone on a network can copy any book from any server to any other server.

This is not like Google Docs where documents are attached to "users" who log into a cloud server controlled by Google. We use cloud hosting for public-facing web pages, but they are all able to be read by anyone anywhere in the world freely without any log ins or passwords. And all these books are created, edited, and shared on the local Pibrary networks hosted on physical

Raspberry Pi based web servers which are shared freely in our local physical community.

Also, we are using "book" as a metaphor. What is a book exactly? How is it different from other media? A book can be physical or digital, can be a private document or public. But what distinguishes it from things like articles or news is that it is self-contained and encapsulates a large body of knowledge in a coherent whole. A book can evolve over time and can get re-written but it has a fundamentally different structure from the news feeds which dominate social media today. Also, we distinguish these books from wiki's like Wikipedia. Wikis are databases of articles. These articles are the fundamental element of the whole thing, and are not organized into book structures. It is hard to write down a clear definition which distinguishes an article from a book, but for our purposes a book is a collection of chapters, each of which is a text document, and all of which add up to some coherent whole.

All books are released by their authors into the Public Domain with no restrictions whatsoever. We do not use the kind of restricted licenses favored by Creative Commons or the Free Software Foundation, but explicitly release books under the Public Domain.

Books, like everything else in the work described here, are self-replicating sets. That is, collections of things which all replicate as a set easily by anyone on the network. The main element of these sets are called scrolls and these are just text documents in the Markdown format. Markdown is a very simple text format which is used in a wide range of online content, which in its simplest form is just raw text, but has a few simple additions like using asterisks for italic, double asterisks for bold, and number signs for headings. While using a markup language like this with a little bit of syntax is in some ways more complex than the completely point-and-click driven editors like Word or Google Docs, this is designed to make the documents compatible with pure-text formats, which is important for making them easy to replicate and edit as we move them freely across our network. We believe that the usability cost of Markdown is worth it for the usability gain of being plain human readable text. The Scroll format used in this work is Markdown converted on-the-fly into HTML using the open source JavaScript library showdown.js. This allows us to set format parameters like font, size, color, and how text fits in a screen using standard web development methods, adapting the same text document to any look and feel or screen size we want(a huge advantage over pdf). This reliance on standard web development methods allows us to have our format work well on all web enabled devices from mobile to tablet to desktop to big screens and of course our free public Raspberry Pi computers without any software other than the browser.

While our primary media format is in the web browser, it is also useful to be able to generate physical bound books, also for free distribution. There are a number of ways to do this, but the one we recommend and are using for this work is LaTeX(pronounced LAY-TECH or LAH-TECH, the "X" is meant to represent the Greek letter "Chi"), and document formatting system developed for the typesetting of technical work. Like Markdown, this is a human-readable text format in which standard text characters are used to indicate to the computer how format will work. For example, while Markdown uses asterisks around a word for italic, LaTeX uses a backslash command "" along with curly brackets around whatever goes in italic. The most important thing about using LaTeX is that for when we create more technical works diving into the physics, engineering and math needed to build the world of full Trash Magic that it makes that easy. This system is already widely used by technology creators and scientists so while it has a steep learning curve it is useful for the experts we are inviting into this system to create technical books. Also, it is compatible with a number of other web-based systems of technical documentation like the Jupyter Notebooks which are an almost universal means of communication now in applied sciences where calculations are done on data using Python or other popular data science languages like R. Another widely used and open source Javascript library(Mathjax.js) allows us to optionally turn on this math typesetting in the Markdown-driven scroll documents as well, so technical books can be written en-

tirely in the Pibrary format and then moved to LaTeX
with the math formatting staying the same.   Conversion from Markdown to LaTeX can be enabled with Pan-
doc, the"swiss army knife" of document formats(see pan-
doc.org for details). Once a book is in the LaTeX format
it is compiled into .pdf in whatever book size is appropri-
ate. We generally use this to compile to two formats: the
letter size in the US or A4 in metric countries for printing
on standard home or office printers to bind in three ring
binders and the 6x9 inch format for binding from print-
on-demand publishers. We use Lulu Press(lulu.com) to
create the bound copies in various formats.

The exact means by which books are replicated will
be discussed elsewhere, but essentially it is all based on
building links to scripts which can be run from a browser
which fetch lists of files and use that list to fetch all the
files. The best way to learn how to do this is by example, and the replication of this work will involve directly
showing people how to do this in person, via video, and
via real time online communication we will be setting up
in the coming months.

So far we have discussed the format of the Magic
Books but not the purpose or what books we will share
first. The purpose of the library of books we are creating
here is to be a repository of all the knowledge needed to
build full Trash Magic. This means we need to create a
culture with everything that goes along with that: history, philosophy, politics, technology, science, math, and

all the wisdom required to be stewards of the land we are a part of. This system of books also needs to self-support. This means that as a social media platform it needs to generate economic value measured initially in money which can provide material support to those of us creating and replicating the network.

The beginning of this library is the books created by the author of this book, Trash Robot. This includes the Trash Magic Manifesto, the Trash Magic Action Coloring Book, and the first Book of Geometron, as well as this book, Geometron Magic. Trash Robot is also in the process of creating another book, Trash Physics, which is part memoir, part criticism of the structure of modern physics, and partly the start of a whole library of physics texts based on the principles here.

The way the library of Magic Books we describe here will become self-sustaining is by documenting the commerce in local communities in a deep and organized way that no existing resource does. This is not just a business directory. It is the creation of a new level of social networking in physically local spaces that does not exist on today's Internet. We will work with local people to create books on local history, local culture, the local economy, the local government, local mutual aid and outreach organizations, local libraries, local religious institutions, and compile all of into books which are shared on our system. Again, this is not a wiki covering existing things. This is a library, creating new deeper connections than exist today, diving deeper into history and culture than the existing Web does. It is also not news. We aim to create new social links in physically local spaces with our system which enable people to engage in new commerce with each other locally. We call these books the Books of the Street, where the "street" here refers to a local public space where we site the Pibrary discussed in the previous chapter.

The Books of the Street are doing more than documenting existing networks and businesses and people. They are *creating* social networks of actual humans in a physical space which do not exist in today's globalized world of cars, planes, and long distance communications. They represent a cultural shift to extreme localization of communities localized to just a couple of miles across, which still maintain the flow of global information across the entire human race.

Creating connections between people which did not exist before can enable commerce. Enabling commerce creates cash flow in exactly the same way it does in centralized commercial social media. This cash flow generated by the network creates a strong incentive for network participants to materially support network creators. Supporting us, the network creators, allows us to spread the network, and if that spread generates more value wherever it goes, that becomes self-sustaining in growth. Initially, this network is simply a social media platform which provides a totally free, non-capitalist (no money, no property) resource to those in the existing capitalist economy. If we can scale with positive cash flow in each local node, this creates a much more efficient scaling mechanism than existing venture capital backed technology startup companies, which generally scale at a loss in order to gain market dominance. Without the billions of dollars of venture capital money required to scale, we can move faster and be more adaptable than those networks, enabling us to ultimately take away all their market share bit by bit from a bottom-up approach.

Consider any "technology" company today which makes its money on creating links between people. From ride share to dating to advertising, all these companies are simply connectors. They connect people with other people and then demand rent from us for doing so. A free network driven locally from the bottom up with community owned hardware and no intellectual property can easily defeat this network one street corner at a time. We can take Silicon Valley down to zero if we can get the right growth model of our network, and it is in the best interest of all people that this happen as soon as possible, since the predatory model of Silicon Valley is destroying us all. We are asking people with great urgency to contribute to this campaign.

A final note on what books we choose to replicate on any given Pibrary. In a traditional library, more is always considered to be better. The more resources a library has the more books they buy, and it is assumed that readers use search and browsing to find what they need with no core specific purpose. This is not the case of the Pibrary. The Pibrary has a purpose, our purpose is to create self-replicating media which can transmit self-replicating technology made from trash which can provide for all human needs for free. We therefore are very specifically *not* trying to just add more and more books. We want the selection of books to be very aggressively curated by the caretakers of the Network to specifically carry out whatever the next task is in any given community to bring all of humanity closer to full Trash Magic. In some cases, this might mean an individual person carries an individual Raspberry Pi with just one or two books, specifically fro the exactly actions of mutual aid and direct action in which we are engaged.

Chapter 5

The People of the Network

We aim to build a network which helps as many people as much as possible. We aim to start by helping the most marginalized people with direct assistance in the form of communication, knowledge and power resources. To support all this, we are building a network which takes back the value generated by the Internet to local communities with much simpler and more human connections based around common spaces. These human connections provide value to different people in different ways, and in this chapter we discuss different roles and benefits that people can get from a local network. The "tech" will end up being incidental. The architecture we are creating is one not of computers but of people.

Big Tech doesn't care about anyone's community. They provide just enough increases in efficiency and human connection between people to get us addicted to their products, then extract all excess value that they can using the power of monopolies to create a vast suction of value from everyone everywhere in the world to the professionals of their industry.

Multiplied by hundreds of millions of communities, this leaves trillions of dollars on the table in commerce which can be recaptured by local communities away from Big Tech. If we can provide more increases in efficiency and more human connection than Big Tech but keep the value in our local communities, we should be able to take every single dollar out of their system, to totally destroy Silicon Valley. Our long term aim is to purge the Earth of them, to totally destroy the culture and society of the so-called "tech industry". We should be able to engage in commerce anywhere in the world without sending a single dollar to California.

This chapter is a recruitment request. We are looking for all these people to join us, to join this movement and this network. We need you to collaborate to share knowledge and resources to help build this. Ultimately we want this network to belong to everyone everywhere, but right now we are directly asking all the people below to reach out and collaborate to immediately bring this network into being in the physical world.

The people of the network. We create this network to support ourselves. We learn to build all the parts of the network, and travel from place to place teaching others to copy the whole system. Ultimately we hope this category includes *everyone*, since if this all scales up all of humanity can live off of the flow of value across our network. For now this is just anyone who knows the system, starting with me, the author of this book. We curate knowledge into Pibrary, build technology kits and give them away, build crafts and give them away, and teach people to copy it all. We can work off of direct donations of food and shelter and resources as well as large grants for community development and education(discussed in a later chapter). Our primary mission is replication: to teach others our ways sufficiently that they can become a fully self-sufficient person of the network.

Public Librarians. The Pibrary is an extension of the library system. The public library mission is make knowledge as free as possible. The pibrary consists of freely created, edited and shared documents on free hardware maintained in public spaces and available to all. Public libraries currently serve as a computing and Internet resource for people with no other access. The Pibrary brings physical computers out to the streets with 24/7 access, taking some load off of the computing resources in the physical library, and extending hours and accessibility of the resource. By being useful for other communities, the Pibrary can be self-supporting, extending the reach and impact of the library without costing money from the base library budget. Pibraries also extend the effective collection of the library, as user-generated content is all completely free and openly shared, replicated globally from one to another potentially over billions of servers. As we scale up, it should be possible for a local public library with almost no budget or resources to have access to a very large collection of free titles. Libraries with maker spaces already have STEM education curriculum and often already have Raspberry Pi's, and this network simply adds to the impact of that, adding content to it.

Authors. If you are someone who writes for the common good of humanity who believes in free knowledge without the limits of intellectual property, the Pibrary can be a platform for creating explicitly free work. As we scale, the intent of this network is to have authors created through direct material support from the communities we serve. If we can get authors generating knowledge to provide all the good things in life, this will be a self-sustaining system without money. Thanks to print-on-demand publishing, it is possible for authors to make money on hard copies of their Public Domain works, and that is the most efficient way for us to make money on this. A book can be sold for 15 dollars where an author makes 7, and people can buy it not for themselves but to release for free into the community as a shared artifact, like a library book. If we are only producing books which people in a local community want to use widely, we can ask people with some extra money to buy a number of copies and give them out. This is the main way I intend to survive off of the network, by selling books. No work may be posted unless you relinquish all copyright to public domain.

People who inhabit public spaces. This includes anyone who does not have access to indoor amenities due to the structural violence of poverty. Ours is a mutual aid based network. This means primarily that we are providing fully free infrastructure and services in public spaces on the streets, directly controlled by the people who need it. This means we will provide free wifi hotspots, free solar powered device chargers, and free easily portable physical computers you can use 24/7. It also means that we will be co-creating documents which have all the resources available in the local community including contact information for aid organizations, jobs, housing resources, harm reduction organizations, and anyone else who is providing resources. It also means we are going to be asking for your help in sharing and growing the network. If our network grows we will eventually be able to make all the things of a good life free for all people, and the only way to do that is to provide for those who have the least first. And the way to do that is to incorporate you directly into our emerging community, where you can actively engage and contribute by sharing your own stories and creations with the other readers and creators on the Pibrary network. For our network to succeed, we must provide the most to those with the least first, and those people must become active partners in our venture.

Teachers. This system can be used by writing teachers to help students co-create published books directly to their local community as an alternative to papers read only by the teacher. It can also be used by anyone teaching people how to code as a development environment which can be run in a web browser, then published to the network and shared with the world instantly without any gate keepers. Rather than learning how to code in a job for a company, we teach people to code by directly building web content immediately and publishing to the network for other people to build on. Our aim is to transition all teaching from job training to direct creation of useful resources for people's communities. The Raspberry Pi can save a lot of money as a low cost powerful computing resource, and the more people we share this with the better.

Traveling kids/dirty kids/crust punks. Think of the Pibrary as a deep sign, or perhaps "hypersign". A cardboard sign, cloth flag with url or QR code can point to a web-based mirror of the chaos books. These books can have *anything* on them. You can share your stories, share whatever you have to share, to sell, etc. By forming connections with other people who maintain the networks and are supportive, you can maintain documents for free online with no gate keepers, no censors, no algorithms, no passwords or logins, just free things to share freely which can help get the information out there that you need to get the aid you need to stay happy and healthy on the road. You have a critical role to play in growing the network, sharing our resources and story with the world. This is a knowledge network, a linking of people who inhabit shared physical spaces. You can help us to link up all the social networks which connect in physical crossroads like downtowns and truck stops across the world. And we can help you by helping to promote direct mutual aid to help you on the road. In a world without property, you are also the pumping blood of our network, moving physical goods to place to place without money.

Scientists, mathematicians, academics. This is a publication platform with no barrier to entry. If you produce knowledge you are willing to share freely with humanity, this can be a platform which not only shares what you have created but which is built in such a way that others can immediately build on it. You can write a totally incomplete paper with most of the important parts missing, and if it gets to the correct collaborators, they can build on it and replicate it back to the network and you'll get back something much better than what you started with. This is a new way of doing research, where we do not associate documents with individual people but with a process of improvement where all readers and writers are co-creating the work over time. We advocate letting go of ego and prioritizing progress over personal accolades. However, this publication is still compatible with career-boosting publications as it can be treated like free online archives are now with preprints of articles that eventually go into gate kept peer review journals. These documents are compatible with the LaTeX system of mathematical type setting, a small modification is all that is required to turn it on.

Off grid experts. Do you know how to work with solar panels, or build small hydroelectric generators? Or how to can and pickle your own food? How to build composting toilets? Organize a community garden? This is your free media distribution channel. This platform is how we can get your builds, your methods, your little tips and tricks out into the physical world into the hands of the people who can use them. We will help organize and curate a collection of your skills and methods into a form which gets the absolute maximum impact. As stated earlier in this work, the replication economy will provide a non-monetary return on your investment, deploying the collective genius of millions or billions of people to take what you have built and improve upon it exponentially and bring back a replication of the evolved document with the better technology.

Keepers of indigenous knowledge. We aim with this knowledge network to bring back a more dynamic living type of knowledge that has existed throughout the world in indigenous cultures for thousands of years. It is our hope that by bringing free computers, free Internet and free off-grid power for it all to communities with posses indigenous knowledge that those people will be empowered to share using this platform, both with each other and with the world. Our network is a hybrid of oral tradition and digital methods, where community members are all co-creating documents which are then passed along freely to the whole of the community. The world today is in urgent need of indigenous science and technology if we are to restore equilibrium between humanity and the living world. The survival of our species now depends on our ability to spread knowledge about how to live in equilibrium with an ecosystem to all of humanity. We need the traditional technology and culture to be able to blend with that of the Internet and computers if we are to navigate the whole of humanity out of our current predicament. Our intent is to get the hardware into your communities, teach your teachers, elders, and other stake holders how to run and grow the system, and then it becomes your network to shape as you see fit. We also aim to have the network of off-grid computers and wireless links connect with environmental sensors, putting the living Earth onto the indigenous network in a very literal way, hopefully giving it more of a voice in the affairs of the our world as well.

Mutual aid workers, harm reduction, street outreach, community organizers.
We can train you to build and share the Pibrary system which will help people charge their devices and get access to the Internet. Also, the Pibrary will have a book

dedicated to community resources which you can both contribute to and share. This can be a directory of links to resources, people, places, organizations, jobs, housing, really anything that is freely available to help people out should get cataloged here and that should be actively maintained by all. Think of this like a phone book for resources for those most in need of those resources(any resources).

People who have too many physical books. You know who you are. You know more than half your books are ones you'll never look at again and don't need but both are not sure which half that is, can't bear the thought of them going into a dumpster due to a library donation drive getting too many books and don't want to lug them all over the place. What you really want is to get them into the hands of an actual reader who will actually read them. We are building a network of places of sharing, and all this centers on knowledge and books. You can use this as a vehicle for finding other readers with which to exchange physical books for free.

Artists. The art you sell does not have to be free, but the media describing it does. This is a platform on which artists can co-create whole books which catalog the art they create and sell or promote whatever commercial channels they use for that. This is not an advertising platform. Spam gets deleted. But it is a place where people can create long form exposition of whatever they produce and place all that in the context of other creators' art and craft products. As with the creations of authors, these books can be sold as physically printed bound volumes from print-on-demand as well as being shared freely online. We aim to create a coherent whole out of all the art created in a given physically local community, to the benefit of all.

Deep readers. The knowledge which can only be attained through reading a lot of books is of great value to a library community. We need people to put together libraries, to organize content, to edit, and to add manuscripts which are already available for free but not widely distributed. We also need people to curate libraries, to figure out exactly what people can benefit from in a given community. That can only happen with very active participation by people who read a lot, both widely and with some depth into various fields. Reading lists are of the utmost importance.

Practitioners of religion/magic/spirituality. The Magic Books we co-create with the Pibrary network are living documents. What better way to transmit wisdom could you ask for? True wisdom does not belong to anyone. True wisdom can withstand the maelstrom of a chaotic co-editing process by potentially billions of readers and writers and end up better than it started. We ask that you consider sharing what you know and what you have learned from your teachers in this truly free form.

Technology creators. One of the core functions of this knowledge network is to spread the technical knowledge required for people to build a new civilization from the waste streams of the existing one. This requires a whole new way of creating technology, based on free sharing of knowledge over this network. Ideally this can be a self-sustaining way to exist in society as a creator of technology. We can create technology, share detailed documents on how to build it, and it will come back to us with community additions much better than what we built. As the network grows and we build more and more truly free infrastructure (manufacturing, housing, food production, power, etc.) we can eventually fully support ourselves off of this network. We will release our creations for free into the network and get back more free stuff than we put in as the network effect accelerates innovation.

Organizers. What is organizing if not creating new social networks? Our network creates shared public spaces for shared public knowledge, and we invite all organizers to use this to create books which help create their own social networks. This can be a political group, a union, or an affinity group of any kind. Rather than a flow of information in a news feed or a "page" in some social media platform, you create books which document the social system you are creating with a greater depth and permanence. This can include a deeper examination of your motives and ideology than would be possible in a shorter format. You can think of this as a manifesto, a constitution, a history, or any other deep form of knowledge which is the basis of what you're organizing.

Local government. This network of documents can be used to create community knowledge which includes the activities of local government, increasing engagement and effectiveness. One of the main goals of creating local networks is to bring power away from central governments and down to the local level. You are responsible for helping to promote economic vitality in your area, and building free public network resources fulfills this mission. As with public librarians, we hope to create partnerships with local governments to get grants for development of the network in addressing issues of the "digital divide". Creating strong local networks can bring in money and jobs and people. As we hone the methods of this network we can provide increasingly tried and tested systems for you to raise money, build infrastructure, and reap the rewards.

Owners of public spaces like shopping centers. Creating a locally controlled network which is free for everyone and which enhances the depth and meaning of a space increases the value of that space in every way. People who own spaces with a lot of businesses open to the general public can collaborate with the people of the network to find business owners and other community members to work with to provide the network access, host the servers, and pay for the domains and cloud hosting. We are building new social networks, new communities which do not currently exist around the shared culture of working toward building full Trash Magic. This common cause will cause excitement and foot traffic, increasing wealth generation for all people involved in the space. As we grow the Trash Factory system, we will need retail outlets for some of the things we manufacture, to both give away and sell, and properties with retail can benefit from this added business.

Art Gallery Owners. An art gallery is already a type of library, as well as a network. It links artists with the public and with patrons. It links art with the rest of the cultural context in which that art was created. And finally it is a physical place, the survival of which depends on how people view its meaning. Building a free book which represents the meaning of the *place* that is a gallery, studio or other art space can act to amplify the value of that place, benefiting the mission of the space.

Role Playing Creators Use the Map Book to create a mixed reality game in a physical space. Games can create complex layers of meaning and experience in a physical space. Work with the people who already inhabit that space as well as other people we draw into the space to co-create new layers of reality using the medium of the Map Book. This project might turn out to be the most powerful in the whole system. Our aim in this work is to create social media which is a hybrid between the physical space our bodies inhabit and the media which defines the world our minds inhabit. This work requires imagination and story telling. If we can engage the imagination of game-creators it can make these worlds much richer and inspire the kind of actions we need to get all the other people involved who will make our network a reality.

Chapter 6

Cybermagic

Cybermagic refers to sets of computer files which include scripts to replicate the whole set as well as both documents on *how* to replicate the set and also on *why* we want to replicate it. We use the term "magic" here to mean sets of things which include the *desire* to replicate the set. The files and hardware themselves never warrant the term "magic". We apply that term only to refer to the property which makes people actually have the desire to choose to replicate the set. It is this human intention which animates technology, and that is what we call "magic".

Cybermagic is self-replicating code which can all be replicated freely from one Geometron server to the next entirely from the Web Browser. We do not "install" software. We use only code which can be run from a browser without ever logging into a server. To make a self-replicating set of computer programs we have some scripts which copy all the other ones, some files which load, save and delete files, and some which catalog them. This set of files can combine with any other set of files, and together can build self-replicating sets of files, where the *entire* set is managed from a Web Browser over the network without ever logging into the server.

This chapter will get a little technical. It is to explain to people who know some things about computer programs how the software here is structured. For those with limited technical knowledge but some interest, we try to describe all the terms in the hope that this can be an invitation to learn all these languages and become a Geometron developer. Email the author with any questions.

Our intent is not to recruit developers into the project of co-creating this system but to teach people from scratch how to work on it, to build a whole new culture of creating software with no link to the existing one based on profit and control. This is a political and social choice. We believe that the work of professional software developers who work either for money or for free but in support of commercial software do great harm with their work and that making a hard cultural break with this group of people is necessary to build system which have more decent human values than those that dominate our world today. For this reason, this chapter has to both be a little bit technical to try to invite people to learn and join us, but not technical at a level which assumes someone is already a developer as it is our intention to avoid working with anyone who involved with the software industry at all.

The main formats of files we copy are HTML, PHP, JavaScript, JSON, and SVG. HTML, or HyperText Markup Language, is the primary language of all content which displays in a web browser. It is the language made up of "tags" which are words or letters between angle brackets along with the raw text that makes up a web document. The language used to talk about HTML is very clearly inspired already by the ideas of set theory, as the word "element" is used to describe all of the kinds of things which exist in a document, like paragraphs, images, links and so on. HyperText refers to the way that documents can all link to each other, making the entire Web in some sense one giant document where documents all link to each other. It is important to note that the "web", based on HTML is not the same as the Internet. An HTML document can exist on a machine not connected to the Internet and much of what exists on the Internet(which is just the network of physical devices) is other kinds of traffic like phone calls, emails, and other data. While the Internet was a creation of the US military back in the late 60s, the World Wide Web, browsers and HTML were all created at the European particle physics lab CERN at the end of the 1980s as more of an academic project. By default, the file index.html is the one loaded as the home page on any given web address. So if you point your browser to a domain name without a file name it just displays this file. We always need an index.html file to exist and replicate for the system to run smoothly.

JavaScript is the language which is part of the HTML standard which does actions, like making buttons or text inputs work, calculating things, or manipulating the HTML content on a page. Whenever possible, our first choice in this system is to use JavaScript for all code that does things because that can exist either in an HTML file(in the "script" tag) or called directly from an HTML file.

The only language we use to interact with files on the servers is PHP. PHP is a old language by web standards(1995). PHP originally stood for Personal Home Page, but it now stands for the recursive initialism PHP: Hypertext Preprocessor. It is a language specifically designed for the task we need: doing things on a web server entirely from inside a web browser over the network. The first and only thing we need to do in order to install Geometron is to copy the program replicator.php onto a web server and run it. That's all! This script calls a file called dna.txt which lists all the other files, and the program uses that list to copy every file in the set. So taken together, replicator.php, dna.txt and all the other files on the server are a self-replicating set of programs all of which replicate when anyone on the network puts "replicator.php" into the browser. This is what makes it incredibly easy, fast, and free to replicate whole sets of documents across our network: it's just links you can click on. All the code in the set is edited using another PHP program called editor.php. This program uses the JavaScript library Ace.js to add syntax highlighting, and loads and saves files using helper programs fileloader.php and filesaver.php.

PHP files are all stored in a directory called "php", and use the file extension .txt so that they can be read in a browser without running them. A program called "text2php.php" finds every single .txt file in the directory php and copies them into a .php file in the main web directory. This can be thought of like "compiling" the program, although it really is just copying the files, and not doing anything else to change anything. The dna.txt file is generated using yet another program called dnagenerator.php.

Data like the list of files to replicate are in the JSON format. JSON stands for JavaScript Object Notation, and is another language clearly inspired by set theory and foundational mathematical ideas. JSON is a minimalist way to organize information into either arrays of pieces of information like text or numbers or name-value pairs which have a name which is just text and a value which can be any of a number of types of information. All these can be fractal, with objects inside arrays inside objects and so on. This format is used for a whole range of different Geometron applications to store data.

All the icons used in the system are in the vector graphics format SVG(Scalable Vector Graphics). These are also part of the self-replicating sets. All of these icons are created from scratch using the Geometron geometric programming language, again all from inside the browser over the network. This shows how self-contained this system is. Graphics, scripts, format, content are all things we can create, organize, edit, delete and replicate again and again entirely from within the web browser over the network. SVG files created with Geometron have JSON embedded in them which contains the Geomtron glyphs used to create the symbol, as well as parts of the Geoemtron Hypercube which are referenced and the style information which specifies how the file is formatted.

PHP programs can take inputs using the text you put into the address bar in the web browser using question marks and ampersands. This allows people to get a huge range of control over the system from the browser, creating new files, destroying old ones, forking the system into new directions on any given server. We use this for instance with a program called copy.php to copy files from anywhere on the network to anywhere on the server we are interacting with. This is also used to create a new file using the editor. For instance we can create a new html file called new.html simply by putting into the browser address bar "editor.php?newfile=newfile.html". Then we can edit this new file, click on the link from the editor to create an updated dna.txt file, and the set which gets replicated by replicator.php will now include the new file. Using PHP programs called from the browser address bar can replace command line operations which we have banished from our system.

This is anarchist software architecture, one of constant chaos. There are no restrictions. Any code can run anywhere any time by anyone. Any file can be deleted by anyone at any time with no log in, no password, just a click and you destroy anything. The same is true for replication. Anyone can copy anything to anywhere at any time. The only restrictions on what is "private" or "public" servers are based on physical network parameters. Local networks can have servers which are not visible outside the the network. This allows for networks of servers to exist in a shared public space, with constant local replication, as well as replication *from* all globally available servers, but without anyone outside the local network able to interact with the servers. One can think of a server only on a local network as having a one way valve for information from the global Internet to the local server. We can build communities of constant co-replication and co-creation of documents over a local network. It is wifi anarcho-communism: a wifi network which abolishes the concept of property, the concept of the "user", all private data, all private code, all private documents, all restrictions on user actions, and indeed the concept of the "self" itself. This is a universe of files without property and without individual identity.

A stripped down set of the absolute minimum collection of files can be useful for understanding the structure. This consists of just the home page index.html, the replicator, editor, dnagenerator, txt2php, filesaver, fileloader, and dna.txt. That set of files behaves like a living thing. It can replicate, evolve, and replicate again. If it is part of an already functioning Geoemtron system, it can also be destroyed by destroying the whole branch it exists on. With servers already in place and human operators already maintaining the system, these sets are like organisms in an open ecosystem we all maintain together. We are not "engineers" who create static technology, but shepherds who nurture and grow a living system.

The sets of files we replicate can include any of a few different file types, each of which has their own self-replicating infrastructure to support it. This includes the image set, which is a set of images people can upload to a server, delete from the server, and replicate as a set. There is also a symbol set replicator which includes the whole Geometron system for creating and editing graphics and saving them to .svg and .png files. There is a generic file set replicator which has not specific format specified. This is useful for files like CAD layout files for circuits or programs other than those in the cybermagic system. One example of this kind of file we will use a lot is the Jupyter notebook, which is a very useful tool for all kinds of science and math calculations and education, already widely used in many fields. As with all elements of the Geometron Magic system, we are creating sets of things which include us, the creators of the sets, and which replicate themselves(with our participation). When these things are computer files, that's cybermagic. With some simple copy/paste it is possible to expand this to any type of sets of files, growing our system to do a wide range of things.

The Map Books are combinations of scrolls and maps which can create swarms of documents which are graphical and text all linked with each other and all of which replicate together. The Map Book can form the basis of physical hypertext documents, which are documents combining maps of physical spaces with hyperlinks to text documents relating to those spaces which can link back to other physical spaces and documents, and so on. Physical places can have physical media pointing to a domain which hosts copies of map books which have links to documents which act to change that space by guiding people to alter it themselves along with the documents. This creates feedback loops of physical media in physical spaces, mediated by our digital media, which can be a powerful transformative force. This mixed reality media can also form the basis of complex games of many kinds, the structure of them is left to your imagination. The Map Book is central to our system! It activates physical spaces and creates new worlds for us to live in. But it is also just a self-replicating set of files like everything else here.

Any set exists at some point on a server and that can fork down to sets in directories, which can fork again and again, making more sets which can be Magic Books, sets of code, sets of symbols, images, or any other file or document. All this happens with a page called fork.html, which allows us to create forks of whatever name we want and replicate the book down a level, and the book can be replaced with any other set using another replicator. Any fork can be deleted along with all its sub-fork instantly at any time by anyone. Everything is fractal.

The only thing that preserves information in our system is constant replication, just like life, which constantly reproduces in the face of constant death. This is living media. We walk the Earth in the physical world carrying our web servers and our physical media and constantly replicate swarms of code and documents from person to person in our physical space. And we remember that the magic is not in the code or machines but in that spark that jumps from one person to the next when we are able to project our desire to build this free network into the minds and hearts of new people. This is cybermagic. Code which carries the media which replicates the desire to replicate the code which replicates the media which describes how to replicate the code, all on physical infrastructure which replicates with us, the People of the Network.

To replicate this system, see the installation instructions in the pibrary Github repository at www.github.com/LafeLabs/pibra

Chapter 7

Geometric Programming

All technology is based on geometry. When a screen displays text or graphics, that is a geometric construction. When we build integrated circuits which form the basis of modern computers, that is just a complex pattern of shapes on a flat surface, yet another geometric construction, as are the circuit boards on which they sit. Architecture is all geometric construction. The paths of cutting tools or 3d printer nozzles through space are geometric constructions. The path of a tractor or harvester going across a field in a sequence of rows is a geometric construction.

Any manufacturing process can be understood as a geometric construction. To build the full Trash Magic we aim for in this work we must create manufacturing processes which replicate from place to place freely over communication networks. If all manufacturing is a geometric process, the most fundamental way to transmit manufacturing processes is to build a language on geometry. This represents a shift in thinking from the dominant machine ideology of today, that of the computer. In the current dominant ideology, the most fundamental things are numbers and arithmetic operations. People think of computers as being engines which use numbers to decide what to do to other numbers. All of the various automation and media functions are considered to be "applications" of this arithmetic engine model.

In Geometron we re-imagine the fundamental idea of machines as always being for doing geometry, and controlled by geometry. This is a philosophical shift, one of values. We choose to value the symbols displayed on a screen and the path taken by a tool for manufacturing as more fundamental than ones and zeros in the arithmetic model.

In computer theory, people have an abstract model they use to describe all computers based on long tapes of ones and zeros which control the movement of the tapes and the operation of doing things with numbers. Computers are then judged in terms of how effectively they process numbers, in a very numerical way, where processing more and bigger numbers faster is a measure of power. This has led to architectures which use an absurd amount of computing power, with machines that do arithmetic operations a billion times a second all to carry out some task a thousand times a second, or even every few minutes. By considering the geometric actions to be more fundamental we aim to move to much simpler machine architectures which will allow us to build machines with less intense technology than modern microelectronic fabrication methods.

We aim to close all the loops in machine fabrication, using a geometric programming language to design and fabricate simple circuits which can run the geometric programs which make more circuits and so on. Rather than trying immediately to build the most powerful machines, we aim to get as quickly as possible to machines which are able to run the entire process of replicating them using their own technology, without any external input. The details of this process will be discussed in another chapter, but it is an essential part of the whole Geometron/Trash Magic process to build these loops of self-replicating physical media.

Just as computer scientists create toy models of imaginary machines called Turing Machines(after mathematician Allan Turing of WWII cryptology fame) which act on numbers, we create a generic toy model for how to create geometric virtual machines. This is called the Geometron Virtual Machine.

In the Geometron Virtual Machine we imagine a tape of addresses, much like the ones and zeros in the Turing

Machine. These addresses represent positions in a pair of imaginary cubes in space, together called the Geometron Hypercube. To make things completely geometric, we imagine the physical tape as having a sequence of symbols made up of arrays of dots, where each pattern of dots represents an address in one of the cubes. Each address in the cube itself contains a tape made up of addresses. So this makes things able to endlessly refer to themselves, since the main tape can reference an address which references another address and so on, building up whole complex networks of geometric actions. Everything is recursive.

The virtual machine can also do physical things based on each address. This is where it is a different model than the Turing Machine. The Turing Machine can be *used* to control physical machines but in its basic model it only works with "pure" numbers. The Geometron Virtual machine has physical operations built into the definition of its structure. Different areas of the address space do different kinds of operation. The details of this structure are covered in the First Book of Geometron. The most basic operation in our system is display of graphics on a screen. This is because the display of symbols is how the machine interacts with the human mind, and again this points to how this differs from the Turing model.

The Turing model ignores the human operator. It imagines an infinite tape which can in theory run programs forever, ignoring the humans who operate it and the physical mater it interacts with. In Geometron the human has multiple roles. It starts with a human pushing some kind of "start" button which starts the main tape being read, and we generally assume the tape is finite and that it only runs one way, once(as opposed to infinite, and running forever). Each address on the tape has a corresponding symbol which is in a human readable format, where by "readable" we mean that it has some clear meaning to the human operator. These symbols are themselves constructions of Geometron. We aim for these symbols to *be* the language used for programming the machines which make all our technology. Different buttons can trigger different different glyphs, which is how we create direct machine controls like "move left" or "move up" for robotics.

Our lexicon of human readable symbols we put in the Geometron Hypercube includes the entirety of whatever written language a human operator is normally using, such as English. For instance, for English we have addresses in the Hypercube for each of the printable letters on the English computer keyboard(which are the same numbers as the ASCII code), and each of these represents a sequence of geometric actions which taken together draw that character. In the current software, this means actions taken in a web browser which control where pixels are in a graphic, a physical construction on a computer screen using the programming methods of the browser. This is called a font, just as in other computer software. A big part of what makes these methods powerful is how they can be mixed and matched with different physical means of geometric action. For instance, a font can be constructed out of discrete movements and drawing of pixels which can be cloned from a robot which impresses dots into clay with a nail to a bitmap on a computer screen to spray paint dots on a wall to microscopic laser burns with no change in the code.

This ability to move geometric construction from one physical fabrication machine to another goes to the heart of why Geometron is a critical enabling idea for Trash Magic. When we build our fabrication technology from parts of machines we find in the trash, having this geometric description of what the machine does independent of the details of the machine makes it much easier to adapt programs from one machine to the next as our system evolves. A program to make a square with a tool which consists of "start drawing, move left, move down, move right, move up" can be done at any size with any tool once we build a virtual machine model which maps those movements to what the motors do.

Of course this is all still based on computer programming languages on machines that do arithmetic. But the purpose of computer programming languages is not just to control machines but to make it easier for our minds to think about how to control them. This is where Geoemtron really does things Turing machines don't, by integrating the process of designing languages, controlling automation, controlling fabrication, and building abstract language structures.

We *choose* to consider geometry to be more fundamental than arithmetic. We believe that this choice is not just a mathematical one but a moral and philosophical one. We believe it represents a shift from an information economy based on replication instead of production, communication instead of domination and control. We use the slogan "no war but the math war" to represent this idea, that we believe that the ideology of numbers is integrated into the ideology of permanent war that dominates the world today, and that shifting away from that way of thinking requires this change in mathematical philosophy. The war machine of today is needed to project power over the long distances required to keep the supply chains flowing which keep material moving from the mines to the consumers. Free replication of geometric constructions in locally sourced trash represents a shift away from empires of control and towards sharing and abundance.

Chapter 8

Symbol Magic

Symbol Magic, like all the "magics" of this work, refers to self-replicating symbols, which people freely copy using the media network we are building. All our media is designed to be created, edited, and replicated entirely in a web browser. The media we use to control *all* machines in full Trash Magic is to be built this way. Be it a cutting tool, a laser, an agricultural robot, pixels on a screen, or any other movement of any machine used to impart form onto matter, we aim to create all the programs to control this in the browser using symbols also made in this system.

As with all our systems, this begins with the ability of the system to create itself. This means we need to be able to make the web graphics used for buttons and links in our web-based media. If you're using this system to read this book, you have already seen these. Using simple square symbols to represent things they link to or actions they cause to happen is a fundamental element of what makes the web work.

We also must now take a moment to define "symbol" in the broad sense used in this work. We define "symbol" to be *any* geometric construction which has meaning to people. This means a building is a symbol. A pie is a symbol. A culvert or dam is a symbol. A microelectronic circuit is a symbol. All of these things have meaning to people and are constructed with geometry. If the materials used to make a symbol are available locally everywhere in the world and the symbol can be replicated from one web browser to the next, those things can all be replicated. If the system of symbols, which we can think of as a language, also impart the *desire* to replicate a thing, that is where the magic happens, where the things can spread freely from one local community of people to the next across the globe.

The language of Geometron in the web browser is more completely documented in the First Book of Geometron. Here we just discuss how it works and what it can do and what we plan to do with it as the system grows.

Symbols used to represent geometric actions are generally in a square. The symbol itself is a sequence of geometric actions. So for instance the action "draw a circle" is denoted by a square with a circle and dot in-

side it. In order to draw that symbol, we must instruct
a browser to draw pixels representing this geometry. We
do that by breaking down the construction into actions
which can be described in a purely geometric way, without direct reference to numbers. For the symbol for circle, for example, the construction is: move to the right,
draw a square, shrink the unit by two, move left and up,
draw circle and dot, move down and right, then increase
the unit by two. This unit is of course some number of
pixels in practice, but the construction uses language independent of the actual value of that unit. This makes
our language independent of specific numbers. It is a sequence of discrete geometric transformations, which can
be carried out with any physical medium at any scale in
any coordinates. This abstraction is incredibly powerful because it means that we can very quickly and easily
create a new implementation in any language or format,
and transfer a symbol over without changing the code.
This is how a symbol designed in a web browser can be
converted to a physical thing made in a laser cutter, 3d
printer, clay printing robot, spray paint robot or microscopic lithography tool.

The basis for all the discrete geometric actions are
scales and symmetries. We do not refer to angles in degrees or distance in pixels, but in rotations and resize operations based on the natural structure of the world. This
means we start with fourfold symmetry, fivefold symmetry and sixfold symmetry. Rotations are combined with

angle manipulations like doubling or bisecting an angle, or tripling, or dividing by three. This approach uses numbers in any given implementation, and can be used to represent numbers but again is not actually based in numbers. The symbols we use denote actions based on symmetries, rather than any specific reference to angles in numbers. The scaling is based on the symmetries. For example, everything based on the pentagon and pentagram have natural scaling based on the Golden Ratio, which is the ratio of the side of a pentagon to the longer distance between points across the pentagon. The same relationship exists for the hexagon and square root of three scaling, and the 45 degree right triangle and the square root of two. So rather than using numbers to re-scale units, we use these universal scale factors based on symmetry, like "multiply unit by the square root of three" or "divide by the Golden Ratio".

We use this system of drawing and moving a drawing tool around to create *everything*. This can be used as a replacement for both art and engineering software, creating plans that people can read to build things with their hands. In its most basic form, it is used to manipulate pixels in a web browser using the "canvas" element which is part of the basic standard available in all web browsers via HTML and JavaScript. We can interact with Geometron with a touch screen, a keyboard, or other hardware interfaces we build based on Arduino. In the touch screen, we work in the web browser as always, and use buttons created out of canvas elements which have events tied to them which control the "Geometron virtual machine", or GVM, which is part of the code in our system. We can also use a keyboard to control the actions of the GVM by putting the cursor in a text input and writing keystroke events which call our code and do things to the GVM and ultimately symbols in canvas elements. This shows how everything in our system points back to itself(everything is recursive). A canvas displays a sequence of symbols, each of which is drawn with a piece of software which replicates with scripts which also run in the browser. This sequence is edited by hitting keys on a keyboard painted with symbols or canvas elements which use the same software to display the symbol of the geometric action in our program. Any sequence of Geometron actions can be called a "glyph".

A Geometron glyph is a magic symbol in the sense that it replicates itself with human control. We edit the symbols which control all our geometry using symbols made of symbols and so on. All this can happen in a web browser using applications which replicate via the cybermagic system discussed earlier in this work. All the information required to make a GVM for a canvas and edit glyphs is contained in a JavaScript library called geometron.js, which we replicate and edit as part of our system.

The software which we use for all the work with canvas elements can also export to the vector graphics format SVG(for Scalable Vector Graphics), as well as the bitmap format PNG(Portable Network Graphics). The icons used as links and buttons in our system are in the SVG format and are all stored in a directory which gets listed and copied using dna.txt and replicator.php in the cybermagic system. These can also be used as technical illustrations and art in books in our system. Collections of these files are in a feed which we generate using web based applications in cybermagic, and these collections are themselves self-replicating sets. Replicator scripts can be run from in a browser on any server which will replicate a set of SVG files from any other server on the entire Internet. This set can then all be edited live in the browser on the new server, and then replicated out to yet another server and so on. This is the power of Geometron Symbol Magic: to have symbols be edited live in any browser on the planet from any server, and then replicated from server to server again and again, evolving freely. Every icon in our system is like this, and can be edited and changed as the system evolves.

These SVG and PNG files are also the basis of physical fabrication. They can be used to create physical objects using laser cutters. This can be done on a wide variety of laser cutters, or they can be uploaded to a print-on-demand laser cutter service like Ponoko.com or a public library maker space. Laser cutters can cut and etch a huge range of materials, including a lot of waste materials. Cardboard, plastic, sheet metal and wood can all be cut into shapes in a laser cutter. This means we already have a system here by which self-replicating files entirely managed from inside a web browser can create physical objects out of trash! This is trash magic! The SVG file format can also be imported into other software used to control machines which make physical things, like electron beam lithography for making very small electronic circuits or embroidery machines for making textile patterns.

This system of discrete geometric movements and constructions can also be used to construct three dimensional files from a web browser. We use several three dimensional web-based file formats to do this. The same canvas element we use for all our two dimensional graphics editing in the browser also has a three dimensional mode which we can control with Geometron for live editing. The format formerly known as VRML for Virtual Reality Markup Language, is now called x3d, and a Geometron glyph created in the canvas can be exported to this format, which can then be imported into numerous types of 3d software like virtual reality, augmented reality and games. There are also web libraries which export to the STL format used by 3d printers. With these standard file formats we can get from the web browser to numerous engineering software systems which allow things designed in our system in the browser to turn into physical objects using numerous machines.

When we build our own fabrication machines from

trash, we control them all using the open source hardware platform Arduino(for now). In order to be able to do all programming from the browser, our system includes the ability to generate Arduino code from the symbol glyphs we create in the canvas element which is printed in a text area by our software and which can be copy/pasted into the Arduino software to load onto the board without ever having to interact directly with the Arduino code. This makes the machines we build much more accessible to far more people than is ever possible in existing systems of machine control. Rather than learning to control a machine with either low level code made of numbers and broken English or some high level system based on specialized applications for some specific hardware, we allow anyone anywhere on the Internet to create, edit and share the glyphs made up of symbols which determine what a machine will do.

As an example we imagine a machine in which a winch is on a rail moving side to side across the top of the wall of a high rise apartment building. We build a language of symbols which denote "move left one unit", "move right one unit", "double unit", "halve unit", and so on, all of which display in a canvas element in the browser. These symbols are also painted on keys on a physical keyboard used to input keystrokes into the browser. A non expert can write a sequence of symbols which create a sequence of physical actions in an intuitive way. Then, if the robot is rebuilt with a totally different motor and control technology, whoever builds the new system only needs to find a way to implement "move right one unit" and so on into the new system and the glyphs written in the old system will work on the new one with no modification.

As our system develops we will replace more and more parts with Geometron, until all of our machines are based on self-replicating symbols, whether they are for communication or fabrication or machines which carry out some other task. Ultimately we will build a system by which symbols are the medium of replication we as humans use to replicate all technology from trash and living material forever. The path into the future of this development will be developed in a later chapter in this work.

Chapter 9

Action Geometry

Action Geometry is a method of geometric construction which uses sets of standard shapes and constructions designed to physically replicate themselves using practical physical media. We can make these shapes from acrylic, plastics of all kinds, thin cardboard, thick cardboard, wood, paper or stone. We design constructions which can be replicated based on a sequence of tracing actions using these shapes, and then since we can replicate the shapes and also use them to replicate the construction, we have a fully self-replicating system. This set of shapes is indented to be as practical and universal as possible.

This is in direct contrast to the two dominant systems of geometric construction, which are classical constructions and analytic geometry. In classical construction all constructions are done using *only* a compass and straight edge. This straight edge is *not* a ruler, it is simply a straight object which is used for drawing lines, and all measuring is done with the compass. In school this is sometimes used along with the protractor and the 30-60-90 right triangle, but it is mostly with the artificially difficult system of just the two tools. The main purpose of these constructions is "mathematics education", totally disconnected from building practical objects. Analytic geometry consists of geometric construction using numbers and equations which describe numbers. It is the dominant method used by most computer systems, including our system under the hood.

These methods of either "pure" geometry or numbers-driven geometry are intended to be as general as possible. Generality is not our goal, however. In all the work here our goal is *replication*. We want to construct things from the most readily available materials which are as easy as possible to replicate. And of course we always want to be focusing on working with trash.

Action Geometry is a system of fabrication from flat trash items, starting with cardboard and plastic. It is also a set of products, the shapes, which can be replicated again and again from any flat and stiff material. We make these shapes from laser cut acrylic, and they can form an attractive and practical "product" for free distribution and sales for donation to promote and expand our system. We can also construct them using classical geometry and cut them out and trace them to replicate them. We create the patterns for the laser cut shapes using the geometric programming in the web browser we use for all two dimensional design in Geometron.

Having made the shape set, the next thing we make is the ArtBox, which is a cardboard carrying case for the tools used to make things from cardboard. The box is itself self-replicating in that it contains the tools used to make another box. Along with a series of rolls of duct tape and cut and taped sections of clothesline, this forms our geometric trash factory which can make arbitrary useful things from cardboard, plastic, and duct tape. The exact patterns and instructions for all this are covered in the First Book of Geometron and are really best transmitted through in person hands on learning.

The primary product of all this, the one we make the most of immediately, is cardboard with geometric patterns on it as a form of media. These patterns can be thought of as both advertisements for the Geometron open(no property) brand. They can also be thought of as part of a generalized game board which is integrated into physical spaces as part of mixed reality games we construct using the Map Book in the Pibrary.

The shapes include a 6 inch by 1 inch ruler, a three inch square, a three inch equilateral triangle, an isosceles 120 degree triangle with a three inch base, a 30-60-90 triangle with a three inch long leg, a Golden Triangle with a 3 inch leg, and a Golden Gnomon with a three inch base.

This set can all be generated in the web browser using the symbol magic system, which can save the SVG files which can print from a laser cutter. This is how we can create self-replicating artifacts from trash in a web browser: design shapes in the browser, save to SVG, and either print on a printer, cut out and laminate or print on a laser cutter, then those are used for construction on trash with a marker, a box cutter and duct tape. Acrylic shape sets and rulers cut out on a laser cutter are a useful physical product to create and distribute in bulk as we scale the Geometron network. It costs about a dollar a shape to get them made at Ponoko.com.

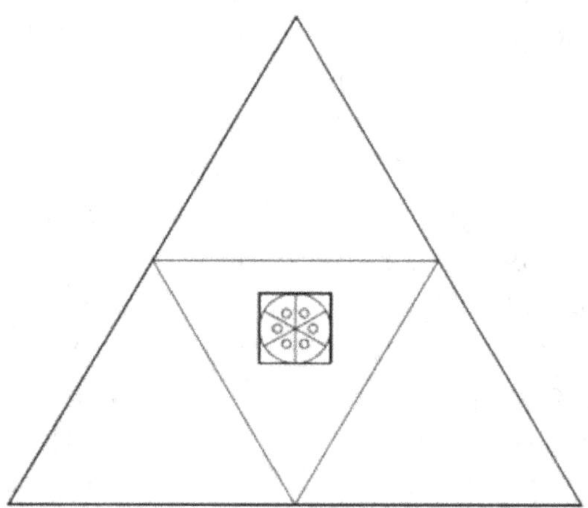

The first shape is the equilateral triangle with a three inch side. Drawn lines are along a 60 degree angle at the half way marks.

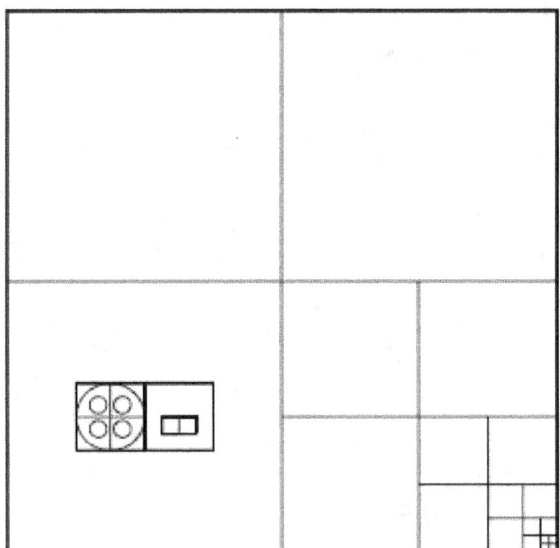

The second set is a three inch square, with lines showing factors of two down from three inches. Just having factors of two from some unit with right angles can be used to make an infinite number of constructions which are easy to repeat. The shape can be used to make another one just like it and each one can be used to replicate arbitrary patterns.

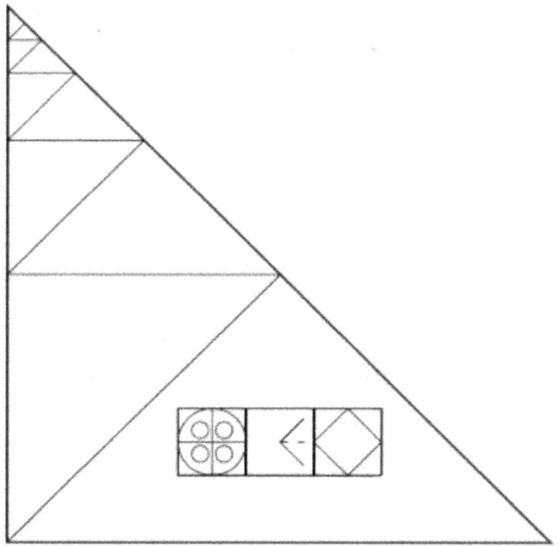

The isosceles right triangle is a common tool in drafting and school geometry and is also one of our most useful tools. What makes our shape distinct from the ones you buy in a store is the square root of two based fractal lines. These are useful for scaling objects by the square root of two, just as we do in the geometric programming in the web browser.

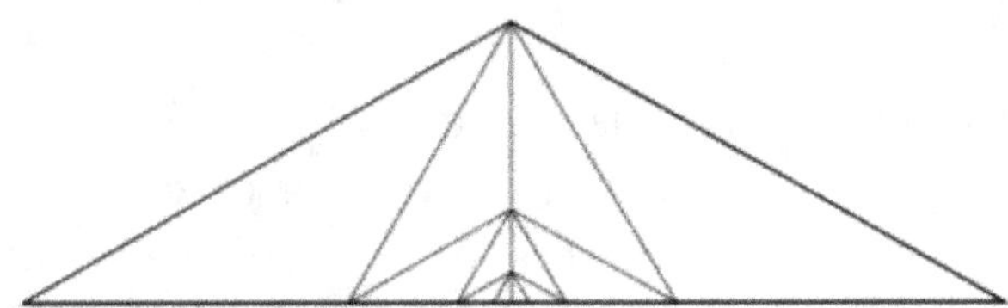

The isosceles 120 degree triangle is another part of our decomposition of the hexagon and all of its geometric elements. This contains scaling lines for the square root of three. The long edge is three inches. This makes it possible to use this with the equilateral triangle to very quickly draw all parts of a hexagon.

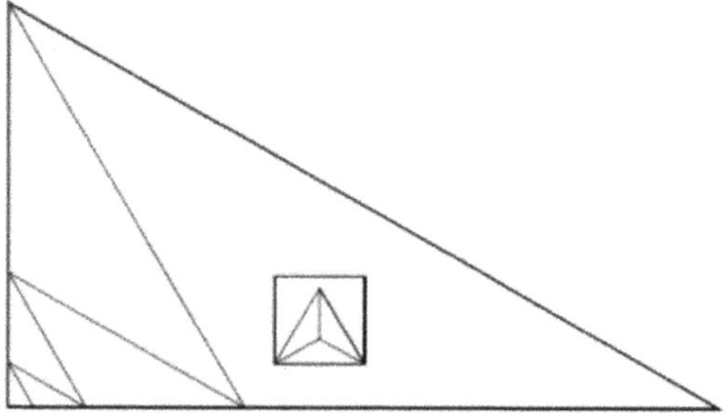

The 30 60 90 right triangle has a three inch leg on the long leg. That makes the short leg three inches over the square root of three, and the hypotenuse equal to double the length of the short leg. Again, this has the square root of three scaling for convenient decomposition of all geometry related to hexagons or sixfold symmetry.

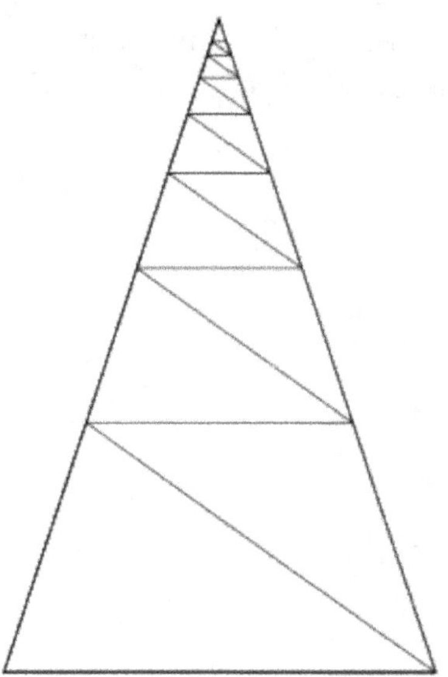

The Golden Triangle is an isosceles triangle where the legs are each three inches and the base is three inches divided by the golden ratio. The Golden Ratio is fundamental to the structure of anything with fivefold symmetry. It is how we get from a pentagon to a pentagram. It is the basis also of all the fantastically complex and beautiful fivefold tiling patterns which can be created with Penrose tiles, and are also present in Islamic geometry patterns. The Golden Ratio is believed to have all sort of wildly exaggerated properties, but it is very useful and can make attractive things quickly. The Golden Ratio is represented by the fractal lines drawn on this triangle. The angles are 36 and 72 degrees.

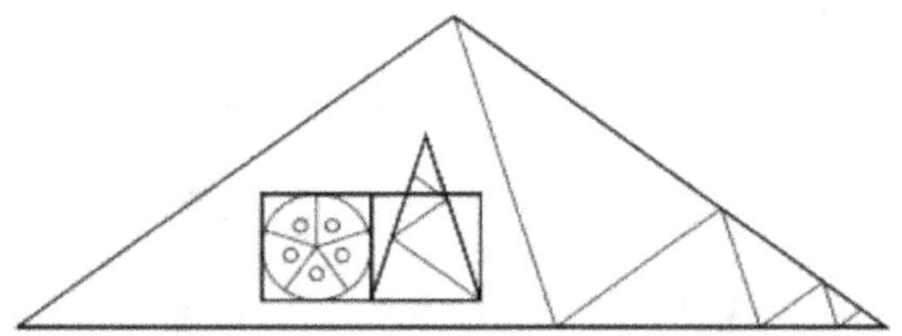

The Golden Gnomon is the other isosceles triangle made from the Golden Ratio, this time with the base being three inches long and the two legs being three inches divided by the Golden Ratio. This combined with the Golden Triangle can make pentagons and pentagrams very easily and quickly just as the other triangles do with hexagons.

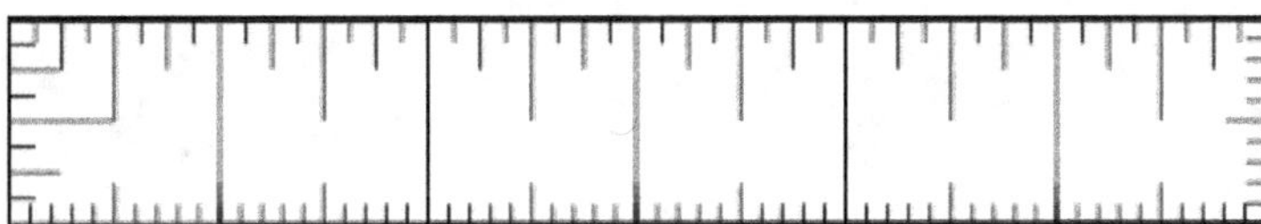

The ruler design we use is a little bit different from most commercial rulers. It is one inch wide and six inches long, and has factors of two on one side and tenths on the other for maximum versatility.

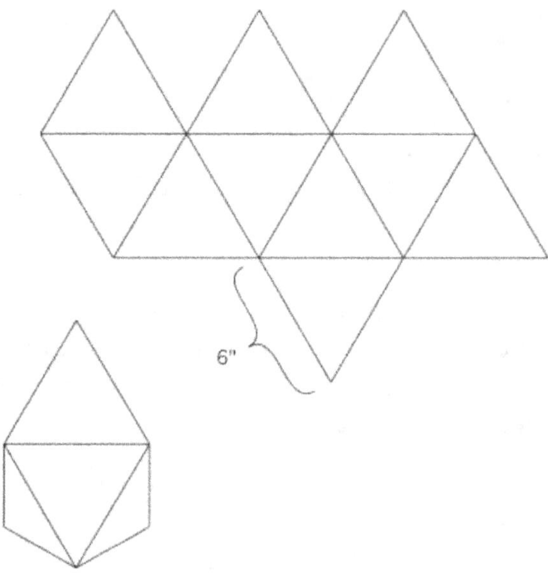

The ArtBox is folded up from 6 inch triangles as shown.

These shapes are all printed out on a laser cutter, cut out of cardboard, or cut and laminated from paper, and then carried around in the ArtBox along with a box cutter, sharpies of various colors, and a pair of scissors. We start making all our cardboard things with making this thing and teaching other to replicate it.

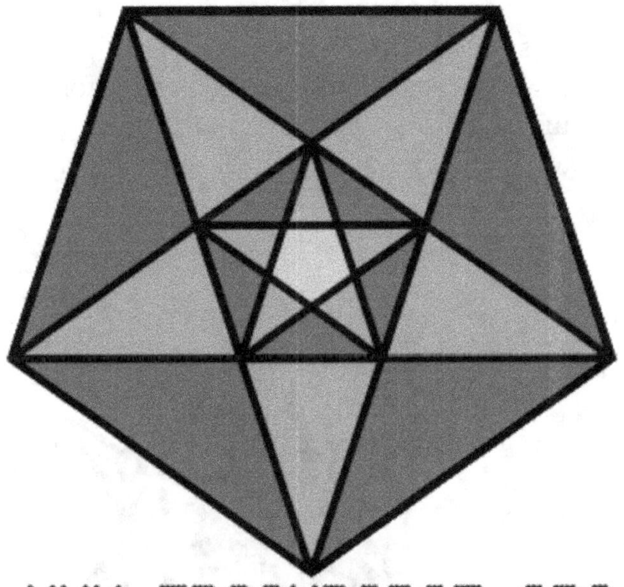

A fractal pentagram colored in.

The pentagram and pentagon are beautiful, and very distinct when drawn with tools versus freehand. A cardboard sign with a fractal pentagram colored in with colored markers is a powerful self-replicating symbol which can be used to spread our memes in the world. We use it to spread our system initially just spreading the domain which points to the main Pibrary of Trash Robot at www.trashrobot.org. These can be made in large numbers with cardboard trash we find on the street or in dumpsters, and can be placed in public spaces as part of our complex mixed reality social media for gaming and community building. These are also boards on which we can place the pieces discussed in the Icon Magic chapter.

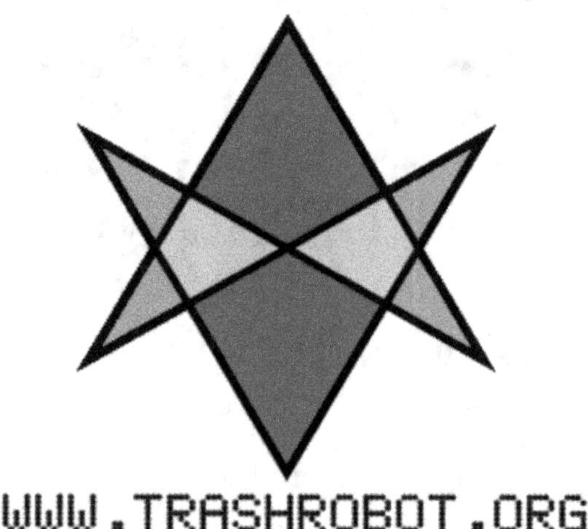

A hexagram colored in.

The hexagram is another beautiful and simple shape which can be drawn easily with our tool set but which is hard to draw well freehand. Again, this is used as an open brand, a sign to draw people in and promote our network, and a generic board for placing other symbols.

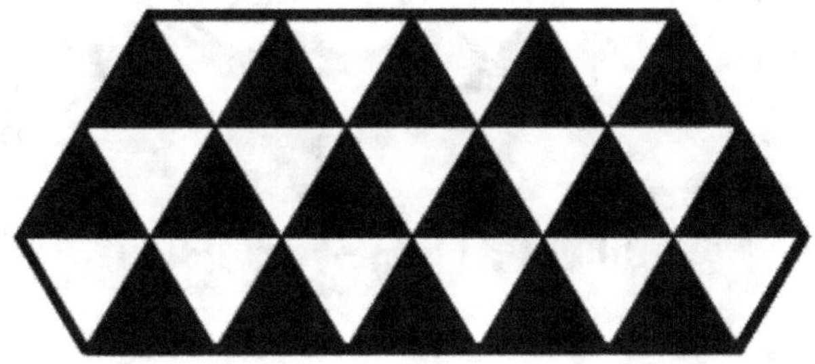

The hex board is a generic game board which can be used for placing generic icon pieces as documented in the next chapter. This can be used as a space for generalized organization of thought. Construct with the equilateral triangle.

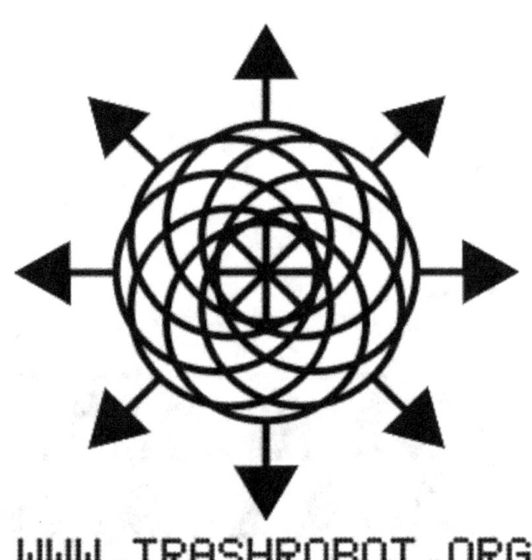

The eight arrows of chaos represents the idea of self-replication in the abstract. This is the symbol on the cover of this book, and when combined with the replicated and rotated pairs of two circles represents Geometron Magic, this book and its contents.

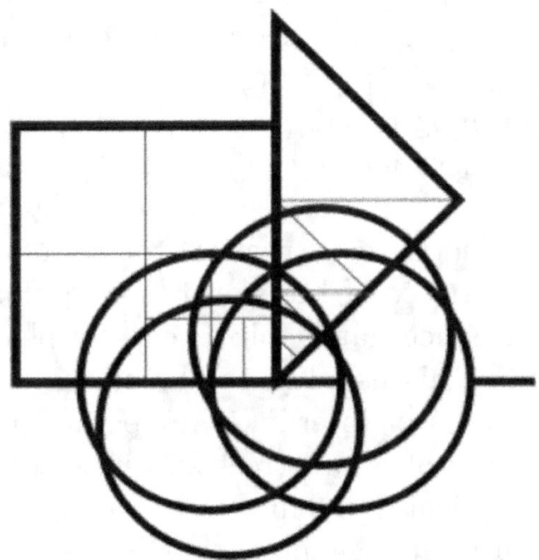

The construction of the Geometron Magic symbol. Each circle has diameter of three inches. Centers of circles are all 3/4 inches out from center. Arrows are drawn with the Golden Triangle. Use a compass, an optional tool of the ArtBox, or a drink lid and create a shape set to match its size.

We also use Action Geometry to make textile crafts, including wearable crafts like shirts and pants and hats which also form self-replicating media, as they are constructed with the tools of Action Geometry and cut out of trash clothing, making lines of clothing which are themselves self-replicating media made out of trash.

Making self-replicating geometric art on cardboard is also a soothing ritual, a form of art anyone can do anytime anywhere for any purpose. The creation of a ritual like this helps to spread our culture and civilization. Many geometric constructions on cardboard spreading along the streets of the world form a global-sized game board on which game tokens can be placed. These tokens will be discussed in the Icon Magic chapter. Complex networks of interlinked maps and text documents integrate the physical street and its media with our digital self-replicating media. The Path of Geometron, described in a later chapter, tells how we will build these Street Books using the Map Book format, on our Geometron Magic book tour.

Chapter 10

Icon Magic

We live in an age when our basic understanding of reality is undergoing radical transformation. We are also facing critical challenges like climate change which can only be addressed by even more radical shifts in our ways of thinking. This means we need to be able to think about "things" in the absolute most general possible sense and to work with sets of abstract things in order to create radically new philosophies which will allow us to undergo the needed changes.

In this section we introduce a general symbolic language for expressing relationships between any collection of "things" in the most abstract sense, using physical media which is part of our system of self-replication. We use this system to design systems of self-replicating sets. So we are creating a system of self-replicating media used to describe self-replicating collections of things. This forms a replacement for money. In a monetary economy, the most fundamental things we exchange are always numbers. Money, stocks, barrels of oil, ounces of gold, and so on are all exchanged in numbers and represent a certain quantity of "using up" a finite resource. We can in some sense think of this as "number magic", since the process constantly replicates the desire to acquire more numbers, to "replicate" a number but only at the expense of someone else. The media which carries all these numbers is generally either private files in private databases or something like the block chain which publicly tallies numbers. But in all cases the numbers are not allowed to be copied. One cannot simply take a column of numbers with 10 units and copy it over and over and give everyone 10 of that thing.

In contrast to this anti-copying property of money, in symbol magic, we are using symbols to denote the sets of things we want to replicate, to replicate the desire of replication. So to do this we need only the absolute minimum complexity required to communicate this desire, and then cause someone we are talking to to put in the effort to go copy a thing. This thing might be an action or a physical object. It might be a huge project which organizes thousands of people to work together or a simple act carried out by one person. But always our focus is the replication of the desire to carry out some physical action. At some level this is a form of advertising, of brand manipulation, and these icons can indeed be corporate logos or brands.

This represents an economic system. Again, in a monetary economy our media is just the list of numbers and people. In this system our media is self-replicating physical media which represents things we wish to replicate. In a monetary economy the fundamental transaction is an exchange of numbers. You get some of one number and I get some of another number, each of us gets a debit of one thing(like dollars) and each gets a credit of another thing(like gallons of gasoline).

In a symbolic replication economy I show you a symbolic representation of a thing we wish to replicate and do whatever I need to do to replicate the replication. That is to say, to communicate to you what you need to go replicate it somewhere else. This might be as simple as a domain or hashtag or social media handle which points you to instructions to copy. Given the Web's ability to create deep knowledge if you know how to find it, this symbolic communication only needs to point to things and replicate intent. The deep knowledge can all be in online documents(all of which also self-replicate).

We present an example of a symbolic replication economy here we call "Icon Magic". In Icon Magic, we create self-replicating Geoemtron glyphs in the web browser which both create symbols in the browser and also create programs which can run on robots made out of trash to print in physical media. We use this with a simple printer robot made of three DVD drives to print in clay using a nail poked repeatedly in an arrangement of pixels. The Icon design software in the browser has a simple system of tracing over images found via web image searches, so that no real artistic skill is needed. Also, the only command needed to create a glyph are up, down, left, right, and the same movements combined with drawing one pixel, so a full understanding of Geometron is also not needed, and this technology can be used by people with no common language or technical skills, just by point and click or simple keystrokes.

We print in Sculpey polymer clay, which can bake in a regular home oven. Once a print is baked, a stamp can be made in it's mirror image with another blob of Sculpey. After this is baked it can be used to stamp out a copy of the original print. This process allows one print to make many stamps and each stamp to make many copies, so one print can replicate out to hundreds or even thousands of copies. This is what we mean by self-replicating media. Anyone anywhere in the world can create a Geometron glyph on any server, which they can then replicate an infinite number of times to every other server in the world. Each one of these can then be printed on a robot which is itself made from trash and documented for replication on all our servers. Each print can then replicate out to thousands of final tokens. These tokens are then painted and sanded, so the paint stays in the dimples, and complex colored symbols can be created this way. Note how this is the opposite of money! Money takes its value from its inhibition of replication. If everyone in the world can copy as many 20 dollar bills as they want, it becomes worthless. But in our system, value comes from replication, and the more people copy a piece of media the more it is worth, because it pumps energy into the rest of our replication system from which we derive all value.

Once these self-replicating icon tokens have been created, we can use them for many things. They can represent objects, people, ideas, places, game pieces, symbols, actions, brands, or collections of any type of "thing" in the most abstract sense. We use them to communicate descriptions of relations between groups of things to talk about replication of things. To do this, we need to arrange them on some surface, and to do that we turn again to Action Geometry as described in the last chapter. We can create a generalized "board" using sharpie on cardboard with our basic set of geometric shapes. This can be thought of as a generalized table top game made from self-replicating media. Self-replicating shapes are used to make the same pattern again and again on cardboard trash, on which the same arrangement of tokens can be displayed and manipulated to communication replication to other people. This physical media is used in a public space covered by the Pibrary. In other words a space with physical media pointing to free domains, along with a free wireless network, free off grid power and free computers/servers of the Pibrary hosting free books which replicate the whole system here.

This connection to the Pibrary is what makes this a functioning economy. If I'm in a high traffic public space with physical media which draws people in and digital media which mirrors all documents to the public Internet, I can communicate all the details of how to replicate complex technology. If I have a space to use our universal philosophical language of Icon Magic on Action Geometry boards to communicate the desire to replicate sets, and the cardboard signs to point people to the digital media, that is a full system of replication. If that system is all on cheap off-the-shelf hardware and self-replicating software, the whole system can replicate. We are building a system where *everything* replicates. In such a system property and money don't really make any sense, because they only function when replication is inhibited.

If such a system produces enough value for people to live on completely, it will create an incentive to transfer more and more material objects into this system. That acts as a force of Nature, naturally transforming property into non-property, and money-based transactions into replication-based transactions.

It is worth illustrating this concept with the mechanics of replication transactions as compared directly with money transactions. Suppose I sit in a public space with a sign. That's the same in both systems. You see the sign in a public space and see me sitting there and come over and sit down and talk in both systems. Now in the money system, we discuss products, agree on a price and exchange money for products. In the replication system, we discuss things which are being replicated, which might be products, actions, ideas or anything. This discussion is mediated by the "game boards" which are used to place icon tokens as if we are playing a game. We can both move them around and talk about sets of things and actions to replicate them. Media can be exchanged in the form of cardboard or paper with addresses of media resources or direct exchange and use of links on mobile devices. Tokens can be replicated with clay or with other malleable physical media(like poured resin or silicone) and boards with more cardboard trash and our basic geometry tools, and the set carried by both parties after the transaction to replicate again and again. So a network of such stations can replicate sets with exponential growth(like a virus) across all of humanity with almost no physical global supply chains. All of this is based on cardboard signs in public spaces, of which there is already a network along all the roads of the world, we are merely adding layers of free media to this existing network.

The various types of clay pieces in the system are all stored in a set of three sewn cloth bags. We think of these bags as having various symbolic meanings, of Earth for the prints, Fire for the stamps, and Water for the final icon tokens we use for communication. So to make our system fully replicating when we are out in public we need all three bags. The prints are used to make stamps, and the stamps are used to make the final tablet sets, which are carried in the "water bags". These bags are sewn from black cotton flannel out of rectangles 8.5x13 inches in size, with an 18 inch black nylon parachute cord sewn into the top as a draw string. The "Earth" bag has a three inch green felt square sewn onto it. Fire has a three inch red equilateral triangle with the point up, and water has a three inch blue equilateral triangle with the point down. We also need sanding blocks or sand paper, and paint pens, and access to a conventional oven, as well as access to a printer robot made from trash and an Arduino, also carried around in a bag. This whole set of physical things can be carried into our public spaces, and used to replicate itself completely with passerby.

The stamps in the Fire bag can also be used to stamp into plastic which is melted over an open candle. This plastic can then be colored in with paint pen and sanded flat like with clay, to make an infinite number of prints with one stamp onto plastic trash. When we combine plastic trash printed with arbitrary symbols with cardboard trash printed with arbitrary geometry from Action Geometry, we have a created a media for expressing any concept of human thought using trash. And this media is physically integrated into a space. Also, all the media points to online resources which link all the parts of the physical space. This is a philosophical language for mixed reality social media.

All this might sound somewhat abstract, and must be illustrated with some examples. The first example is replicating the system itself. This means we just want to have icon tokens for each thing discussed in this book. For example, the Raspberry Pi, solar panels, batteries, flags, and so on. Each thing in this work which has enough of an independent identity in discussion that it's worth talking about gets a symbol. We then make generic boards which are just attractive geometric patterns which put some kind of structure on the cardboard and give it that distinctive geometric pattern which is easy to recognize.

Another example is just game pieces, which are actual physical products with value which are replicated along with everything else. We can make self-replicating chess sets which are carried in a bag and used on cardboard chess sets with sharpie based squares. Each chess board can act as an Action Geometry shape to replicate and make another chess board on more cardboard. As with all sets, we have three bags, and can use the prints to replicate stamps and the stamps to replicate pieces. So one printed set on a robot can create thousands of fully functional chess sets, and whole networks of people replicating the sets, playing chess with them, and replicating them again.

We also use the tokens as game pieces in the mixed reality environment, placing them in various locations in a public space. This mixed reality can involved cardboard with geometry and web addresses, hash tags or contact info and game tokens, all left in public spaces linked to by public facing web pages. This represents a complex network of media which is always a hybrid between physical and digital and all outside of the property system, left in public without any personal possession. All of it is self-replicating, as pages all replicate from server to server, tokens replicate with clay and cardboard replicates with Action Geometry.

We may think of this system as a philosophical language, a universal system for representing structures of human thought. This is something that various philosophers have worked on in the past, but our goals are different. When philosophers like Gottfried Wilhelm Leibniz worked on this problem the goal of all that work was still to express "truth". The goal of both philosophy and science in that time was to create as many statements as possible which were as true as possible. This is not our goal. Our goal is to create the collection of information which taken together allows us to create a fully self-replicating system of technology from only trash, the sun, water, and the living Earth for all people to live a good life for free everywhere. We will create the structure of our linguistic and philosophical tools around this.

We have created a universal symbolic language as a tool for creating a new mode of human existence based on replication instead of mining. This is not exactly "technology". This system is philosophy, it represents an approach to interacting with each other and with things, not a specific technology. It could easily be replicated using methods from thousands of years ago with clay and sticks. Indeed, we can probably think of early human stone tools as examples of self-replicating media in this way. When the first people figured out stone tools, in order for that to replicate enough to have a global impact on humanity they have to travel in a replication economy. One person chipping stones in one creek bed with one special type of stone doesn't scale. A culture of stone-chipping replication does scale. And each spear with a stone point is media which advertises its own replication. Its product in the form of animals to eat naturally replicated the desire to replicate the thing.

This type of media and economy was consumed by the mine system everywhere in the world as the mine-users created machines of war, used them to get more land for more mines and competed to keep doing that until the whole world is one giant mine feeding one giant war machine.

This book must itself be part of a self-replicating set using Icon Magic and Action Geometry. Every single thing described here must be replicated this way, including this book itself, which documents replicating all the things. Everything is recursive in that it points back to itself by replication. Replication can be thought of as a type of ritual. Rituals are sequences of actions with meaning. We will integrate the rituals of replication into existing cultural frameworks by mixing whatever is already replicating in a given community(religion, culture, customs, commerce) with the replication of Trash Magic and Geometron. We do this by representing all the things already in existence in any given community in Icon Magic, and creating ways to represent those things using tokens on boards. This can include religious ceremonies, divination and performance art, business deals, relationship and network building, art projects, games, buying and selling, or really anything anyone might possibly want to do.

Language is how the mind parses reality. Therefore the most fundamental thing which determines how we connect our minds to reality is the structure of language. Building a symbolic language the sole purpose of which is to create a replication economy on trash, the sun, water and the living Earth represents a shift at this deep level where our minds connect to reality. Doing this with cardboard and sharpie puts this linguistic tool in the hands of the people we need to help the most, those who are the most marginalized. This is a language in which mutual aid and direct action are hard coded into the structure by making everything free, focusing on those who have the greatest need, and directly and freely replicating whole system again and again. If this language is able to replicate along with this network, we can consume the old economic system of money, mining and property as fungus consumes a log, turning all these things into new things which can stay put and cycle materials freely forever.

Chapter 11

Full Geometron

We will make everything from trash, without exception. We will abolish all global supply chains and mining and make things using only the materials in our immediate environment. Our media will be outside the property system, merely a shared resource which we use to replicate all the things in our replication-based economy of trash and sun. However, all this will take time. Decades. We have to start somewhere.

We must start with the minimum required to have media which is not property and which can carry the knowledge needed to replicate itself. That is the Raspberry Pi and the associated systems described in this work. However, in order for this to get where we need to go, it has to have a *path* forward to full Trash Magic. We do not have the resources to do the whole thing at once, nor would it be desirable to do so if we did, since large intense efforts tend to create systems which continue to require that form of effort.

The first phase of the network described here is enough to start, to get natural replication without any external input from grants or startup capital. The Raspberry Pi can be used to make social media which generates sufficient value both inside the marketplace of money and property and outside of it that it should sustain growth. When this growth starts to ramp up, however, it will pull more and more materials and energy into the network naturally. The natural next step after the Raspberry Pi is to start pulling in more mainstream hardware platforms. This system only needs a web server and the language PHP to work and it can be replicated. This can be done on Windows, MacOS, iOS, Android, and any type of Linux. So ultimately the number of servers can get up into the billions once these start getting switched from private to public use.

Any given server added to our system of common media adds a certain amount of value to a local community. When that amount of value is perceived as being greater than the price of a thing or the value of the thing to its owner, people will naturally start moving hardware from the property system to the Geometron network. As with all network growth dynamics, the value will continue to increase exponentially with the number of elements on the network. As we cross more and more thresholds of value, more and more hardware will transfer over.

Of course, the Raspbery Pi and all these commercial off the shelf machines all still come from a mine. They all still have a finite life time and are deliberately designed to be unusable after that lifetime. In some sense using them doesn't solve any real problem of Trash Magic as they still are all bought for money from an unsustainable system. The next step in our path of conversion is to start using a wider range of hardware so that more and more waste can be used in our system which was on its way to the landfill. To do this, we must turn to the "Internet of Things". This jargon term is used to denote putting computers in poorly designed products which should not have computers in them. Generally they solve no real problem and are designed to break as fast as possible with no possibility to repair. However they are a fantastic resource for us, since they all have to have basic Internet capability by definition.

Our task with these devices is to develop processes which are easy to replicate which remove everything that is not needed from these machines, remove all proprietary software and all the hardware other than the basic Internet connectivity parts, and put a stripped down operating system the sole purpose of which is to host Geometron documents. As with all tasks like this, the way to do this is with a fork of Linux based on other forks designed for this kind of task. A perfect example of this already widely in use is OpenWrt, which is widely used for making routers useful for all sorts of things.

The path above is sufficient to build our global media network outside the system of property, which can be used to replicate things made from trash, while still feeding off the existing extraction based system. We now turn our attention to the ultimate goal of freedom from that system.

All of our modern electronics comes from a vast and powerful web of supply which is very centralized, very brittle, and very unsustainable. Huge quantities of sand with special properties are extracted from the few places in the world where they can be found and transported with oil thousands of miles to the few places in the world where microfabrication happens. This sand is melted in specialized furnaces into giant crystals of insanely pure silicon, which is sliced into wafers. The wafers are then put through a mass production process where each wafer has thousands of chips and each chip has billions of transistors and other components. These combine to make giant arithmetic engines which have clocks pulsing as fast as possible, generally billions of times a second. All the functions of our "computer systems" are based on this very fast arithmetic engine. This all looks a lot like replication, with many dice being stamped out which are identical to one another, but it's not quite the same. They are replicated, but the whole system is not freely replicated. Intellectual property, control of supply chains, and access to the vast amount of capital required to build these multi billion dollar facilities all make it so that the *system* is designed not to replicate.

We must build a new fabrication system from the ground up if we are to free ourselves from the mine and oil system. To do this, we rethink the purpose of the machines we are building. We do not want to do arithmetic. We want to do geometry. We want our machines to do the absolute minimum work required to make the things we want to make and to display information to humans. Furthermore, everything we are building is designed to be controlled directly by humans. When a device is not being used and not carrying out a fabrication task it should do *nothing*, take no energy at all. When a media machine is displaying a static document, the pixels should be energized, and nothing else. All action is initiated by a human, and leads to response not based on clocks but on direct sequences of actions which take as long as they take.

We do not realize how large the inefficiencies are in our current systems because they have seemingly blown up overnight and we have nothing to compare them to. Also, they grew up in parallel with advances in the fundamental science, so we have no perspective on what is possible with today's science given advances in understanding of things like organic semiconductors or various exotic materials which did not exist in the mid 20th century as the current system was evolving. Also, the growth of the current system involved vast amounts of extraction to get the various special atoms needed to create novel electronic devices.

But our whole situation is vastly different now than in the 20th century! Because of the trash feed, we now have every exotic atom available locally to every single person on Earth. Wherever any of us are right now at this moment, there is a pile of electronic junk which is all identical in its atomic composition and which has every exotic element from antimony to zirconium not only available but in a well understood and perfectly repeated format. So while it might be *difficult* to figure out how to use some exotic atom found in a trashed television, in a replication based economy we only need to do it once and then push that media out to the global feed and the whole world gets it for free with no supply chain at all. This is a situation totally unlike any that has ever existed in human history! We cannot possibly overstate the power of this situation. Even if our civilization totally collapses, any future civilization which evolves will always take this as a starting point, will not have to mine to create whatever they create. The product of a globalized consumer society cannot be undone: the redistribution of atomic wealth is permanent.

Also, our economic constraints are totally different than those under which the technology we wish to replace were constructed. The economic forces which created our existing microelectronic fabrication systems always favor size, power, and speed, at the expense of the ability to repair anything. The faster the chips produced go to the landfill, the more money the factories make. The more money they make, the bigger they can get, which lowers price, which makes them go faster and so on. We now aim to break that cycle and build much simpler and slower things which we can repair indefinitely. If an artifact is intended to effectively last forever, being repaired and re-purposed and reused indefinitely, with all the atoms staying in a physical locality permanently, we want to shift from mass production to craft production. We no longer need chips to come out of a factory by the billions or to all be the same and have no defects. If a single circuit takes months to build and requires a skilled craftsperson, that is acceptable to us as long as that circuit can be kept in the community for many decades or centuries. This represents a totally different culture of creation, in which circuits are made directly by communities for their own benefit, but based on knowledge which replicates freely across humanity on the Geometron network.

So what is all this for and how will we build it? We primarily want to do two things: control the machines that are used for physical fabrication(printers, 3d printers, laser cutters, milling machines, lathes, etc.) and control the screens which make up the media. We do all of this with Geometron. In Geometron, machines manipulate units of geometric action, and then use those units to do physical things.

We first look at what this means for fabrication machines. In the current system, all fabrication machines are based on Arduino. The Arduino is a simple open source hardware system. It is easy to buy, cheap, and easy to program. To program the Arduino with Geometron we simply create functions which do geometric actions, and build a geometric instruction set which controls those. So for example with the robots built out of broken DVD drives we use for clay fabrication, the function has actions for moving left, right, up, down, forward, and back by one unit, actions to double unit and actions to halve unit, and nothing else. Programs are simply sequences of these actions. Since these are just geometry, they can also be translated to meaning in a canvas element of a web browser, and connected with symbols which are both displayed in the browser and painted on keys to be programmed with a physical keyboard. This is how we are able to program robots in a web browser with no arithmetic. The universal nature of geometry allows geometric programming from a browser to turn into a sequence of actions on a robot which then turns into physical things, forming a replication technology of those things.

To make complex things like printed characters in a human language like English, we also create a Geometron Hypercube which allows some actions to consist of sequences of actions. So for instance "draw the letter A" will translate to a sequence of "draw a pixel" actions, and each of *those* actions is itself a sequence of actions to move a tool in whatever way is needed to draw a pixel, like poking a nail into clay or lowering a drill press to drill a hole. In the Arduino, this Hypercube is expressed using strings made up of letters. The Arduino, like all Geometron Virtual Machines, takes a tape of geometric actions in this case represented by letters and does something, in some cases another sequence of letters which can in turn call more sequences of letters, and all of these sequences are just strings. Programs created in the browser will generally have a text area on the screen which displays the Arduino code which has the correct strings for the program. This is then copied into the Arduino, uploaded, and we complete the connection from browser to machine.

This system can be used to control *any* fabrication tool, and part of creating our own new way of making things is to close that loop in all cases. We need to be using pure geometric programming in a web browser to control the tools which fabricate circuits, metal machines, metal molds for plastic parts, cut wood parts, moving biological samples for synthetic biology and indeed *every* fabrication task. All fabrication is geometry. All geometry can be expressed in sequences of actions defined using only geometry and denoted to humans using only symbols also created geometrically in a web browser. Therefore it is possible to use the Arduino and Raspberry Pi to build up a new type of web based self-replicating technology.

However, as with the Geometron server, we note that the system based on Arduino is still reliant on the mine and oil cycle we are trying to escape. To escape this, we first need the Arduino based fabrication machines to be making microelectronic circuits. This can be slow. It can be crude, with large devices initially. But ultimately it is the start of the process to replace the whole system with full Trash Magic.

What we want from the hardware which replaces the Arduino is just movements of motors with timers, and a hardware implementation of the Geometron Hypercube and Geometron Virtual Machine. So we want a physical medium of some kind to have information encoded in it in a way which triggers a set of switches which choose what thing happens. This can be purely mechanical, or combine electrical and mechanical, and even biological and chemical or fluid mechanics. All that is needs to do is map states of the incoming tape to periods of time of some state of the actuator which moves a physical thing. There are probably in practice many ways to do this. It could certainly be done using a primitive copy of existing technology, based on silicon and deliberately added impurities. But that is probably not the most effective path. We have learned a *lot* about organic electronic devices, biological and chemical systems, and even mechanical design in the last hundred years and we have no idea how many simple solutions to our problem will present themselves until we try.

Always, our goal is to keep in mind the basic notion of turning physical media on the incoming glyph tape into geometric actions. There is already significant precedent for doing this without modern computers in the automation systems of the early 20th century. But again, what we are doing is much easier than what they did because we no longer need the extremely large scale, we are only trying to build systems which move 2-5 motors relatively slowly doing simple things for craft-based production.

Once we can make our own circuits from scratch using found trash materials which control motor motion, we immediately make sure this can be used to print the physical media which forms the incoming Geometron glyph tape. This basic system, where we replace the Arduino with our own circuits, use those to make fabrication robots which print the code which prints the circuits which makes the robots and so on, we have started to fully close the media loop. If this is done using prints on clay, and those prints are used to fabricate human readable media, machine readable media, and circuits, that closes all the loops. We then want to move from that up to screens, by building electronic circuits the sole purpose of which is to control what pixels light on on a screen when, again with purely geometric programming. This is the final step in full Geometron. When we can control old trashed screens from the existing system using circuits we can make ourselves from scratch using robots we make with that same technology we have a fully self-replicating trash based media which requires no mines or global supply chains. If this media carries all the code to control all the machines to build more media we have full self-replication.

There are many steps left out here. Not all media will be discrete geometric actions. We also need to be able to display bitmaps and play sound. This means we need physical media which directly stores those, which will mean going back to more analog media using our physical media fabrication. Digital media as an alternative to analog media is *primarily* a tool of domination and control. When media is part of a giant system of arithmetic, the only added "value" of that is that it makes it possible to impose controls on what can or cannot be played. Returning to analog, and then combining that analog with discrete geometric controls of where it will get displayed as well as direct human controls seizes power back from the people who have used computers to dictate and control our lives. The machines we are building here are not "computers". They perform the same functions as computers but we use different metaphors to describe them and that totally changes how we relate to them. Removing computers from our lives is a political act, and we cannot do it soon enough!

This fully self-replicating trash-based media is then used to carry the evolution of our other systems, documenting the research and development process as we approach our final goal of building everything to provide all human needs for free for all people everywhere from the sun, trash, water, and the living Earth. This might sound outlandish, but as we hope we have shown, it is not. Each step in this path is something straightforward which can be done using simple experimentation with already-working technology. No miraculous new technology is required here, like molecular nanotechnology or strong AI. This is just a choice to build a new culture and a new society based on a shared value set. It is not really new technology, and that is why we know it will work.

Chapter 12

Community Actions

This is a book of direct action. This is not an appeal to authority or an agenda or policy plan for existing organizations, but a framework for directly choosing to go build what we need to build. Some of the things we need to build will take millions of people decades to build, and will require vast organizations which we can scarcely even conceive of today.

All of this starts with simple direct actions using only the resources we have available to us right now. In this chapter we go through the things we are asking as the creators of this work in order to grow this new economic system to the scale needed to solve global problems. This requires a delicate balance between finding the *right* people with specialized skills who can build complex machines and dedicate their lives to creating new social structures and spreading our message and philosophy to a broad enough audience to provide community support for our core of creators. We begin with the small steps that everyone can take. This is magic, as defined in this work: the replication of desire to build this world, nothing more and nothing less. Without this, nothing else will work. And if we get enough people to believe, we can do anything.

To spread these ideas, this book itself must replicate as broadly as possible. This means we want the free digital form in as many formats and languages as possible on as many web pages and computers as possible, shared with as many people as possible. We also want the physical bound copies from a professional printer to be distributed as widely as possible. This is where the author's self-interest must be publicly declared: the most straight forward was for me, the author, to live off of this network is for people to buy so many of the physical bound book for dollars that I can live off it. If I can live off of book sales, I can work on more books without any strings attached, and this will maximize my ability to push all this work to the next level without distractions. Physical copies need not be purchased, they can be printed and bound yourself, by printing the letter size pdf and binding with a simple loose leaf or spiral binder. Purchasing books is both to get higher quality bound volumes in a smaller format and to support the author. Also you can be Trash Robot. And then we are Trash Robot. Trash

Robot is an art collective, and anyone can print and sell books without any permission or payments. Just ask us how.

We are looking to saturate certain physical spaces with these ideas in order to activate those spaces into our network. To do that, we ask people to buy or print as many copies as they feel they can and distribute them for free in public spaces where we aim to spread the network. These books are not property. In addition to being free of copyright since they are all published on a Public Domain license, we are asking you to never claim the physical volumes as property but to release them into the commons as well. All of this is tied to the other physical elements of the network. Our network is built into the physical street, with physical media and computer and network resources all focused along some area. We look in that area for anyplace that can naturally hold public books and drop books there. This includes libraries, book stores, coffee shops, waiting areas of medical offices, lobbies of apartment buildings, art galleries, schools, religious institutions, break rooms in work places, infoshops, "little free libraries", hotel rooms, and community houses. All of these are strategic placements. We are always using the placement of the book not to simply find readers at random but as a campaign to activate a specific place, to build a new emergent network of people in that space who share our common purpose. We aim to place many copies within a couple mile radius of a location, rather than broadly distribute, and always the distribution is a means to an end, where we aim to expand the other physical elements of the network(media and machines).

Beyond the message carried in the book, the next thing we are asking from people who wish to replicate these ideas is the replication of the other physical media, which point to the digital media. The simplest physical media is the patterns we can create using Action Geometry as a ritual artistic practice. The simple geometric shapes described in the Action Geometry chapter can be created for free paper, pen and scissors(or even careful folding and tearing). These can be used to create a whole universe of tiled patterns which can be used to spread the idea of self-replicating geometry. These are very recognizable, and create a sort of brand identity which can be on any media. This media can include cardboard signs held by people on the side of the street to wall murals, tattoos, chalk art on sidewalks, sewn patterns on clothing, Easter eggs on circuit boards and microchips, computer games, game boards, and really any new type of media we can think of. Any pattern created with this system can be easily replicated by anyone using the same system. This transmits not just symbols but the *idea* of using geometry to make self-replicating symbols. That idea is the most important part of this, since it is the "magic" which drives the whole system, the replication of the desire to build this world of freely replicating things.

As with the books, these geometric patterns which can freely replicate will have the most impact on the growth of our network when they are displayed strategically in the physical locations we wish to activate into the network. These physical media elements point to our digital media which describe the system, including the digital version of this book. This can be as direct and physical as a cardboard sign next to a Raspberry Pi or it can be a sign pointing to a web address which hosts our collection of Magic Books which spreads the network.

Fashion can be one of the most powerful forms of self-replicating media. Shirts, pants, robes, dresses, skirts, cloaks, hats and accessories can all carry self-replicating geometric arrangements of shapes, where each instance is constructed using the shape set and construction methods of Action Geometry, and where the whole is used as a brand identity to spread the core message of our network. If we use clothes and other cloth products which are discarded or donated, this further promotes our message through direct action: the article of clothing both embodies an ideal and transmits a geometric pattern which represents that ideal. Furthermore, developing a tradition of creating extremely recognizable fashion based on our ideas and methods creates a very obvious identity in which we can recognize each other and be recognized in public, creating a more freely replicating culture. This fashion culture also plants the seed for the full Trash Magic textile production we will produce in the Trash Factories when we start to establish more substantial industrial infrastructure in our system like mills and looms which create cloth from plastic bottles and industrial sewing machines creating patchwork trash cloth for use in new clothing and shelter products. All of this clothing production, like everything we produce, is a hybrid of mutual aid directed at the most marginalized people and commercial products sold to support our ongoing operations.

All this can start simple. Just a t-shirt with a couple stitched colored triangles with some obvious symmetry can require minimal skill and effort and no money to make, and can be enough to start a conversation which leads to spreading these ideas.

The next replication action we ask of the reader is participation in the symbolic economy of Icon Magic. This means designing, creating, and replicating the small pieces of physical media which carry the simple pixelated designs of icons drawn as Geometron glyphs which are described in the Icon Magic chapter. For these to freely replicate, they must be distributed and used in a way where the clay prints and stamps are carried with their finished products, so that more can always be made with more clay. The "factory" to produce more of these consists of just a block of polymer clay, access to a conventional oven, paint pens, and sand paper. There are numerous other ways to replicate them, stamping symbols into heated plastic, or casting pourable materials like epoxy resin, silicone or chocolate. As long as the original prints are available to make stamps, we have a system which can replicate an ever-increasing flow of media.

These Icons can be used for many things. In all cases, however, as with all the other media presented here, their primary purpose initially is simply to replicate the desire to replicate the system. So we design them based on what we think people will care about for *anything* they might already care about. They can be board game pieces, markers in public spaces, white rabbits which are to be found and direct people to online resources, used like cards or rune tablets for ceremonial purposes, used for all sorts of rituals, turned into jewelry and worn(earrings, cuff links, belt buckles, pendants, buttons), used as barter tokens for goods and services. As discussed in the Icon Magic chapter any "thing" in the most abstract sense be it an idea, object, person, place, action or set of other things, can be represented by these pieces of self-replicating media.

Participation in this economy starts with simply accepting the physical media from someone who already has them and passing them along. As with all our media, this is not property, it is intended to flow as fast as possible from person to person to replicate all our ideas and culture. Simply take and give, carry and share.

The next level of complexity from simply sharing the Icon Magic media is replicating them yourself. This means learning the clay craft, which you can learn from someone who already knows how to do it, and repeating it yourself. Even easier than learning the clay craft is learning to design your own icons using the Geometron software on any given Geometron server. This can be done on any Raspberry Pi server, and the only product is a sequence of numbers which forms the code for the Geometron glyph which is printed out by the printer robots made from trash. This is just a text string, and can be copy/pasted via text, email, or direct replication from server to server across our network. Creating these icons can also be done by free commission, where you think of a symbol and ask someone who already knows the system to make it. This simple act of thinking of a symbol you want is one of the most valuable in the growth of our system, as it is the signal which determines how the system focuses on what people care about. This act is as simple as asking a robot operator to create a symbol.

While these pieces of media have many purposes, we must always remember that our objective of making everything free for everyone requires that we always provide resources to those who have the greatest need in any given community. This means that directly selling all these self-replicating media can and should be used as a way for people with nothing to support themselves. If people on the street who need money can sell media which they can replicate indefinitely, they create a sort of mutual-aid based currency, in which the thing they sell to someone with more money and resources then represents the information that someone was helped, which can be transmitted through the rest of our social network. Initially this looks a lot like a currency, like money, even though it is *not* money. It is not money because it can be freely replicated by anyone, and because each icon *means* something. Money is designed to *not* replicate freely, and to represent only number. This is designed to represent a "thing" in an abstract sense which is *not* number, is an expression of a Geometron glyph which is pure information, and can replicate and evolve forever.

We can make practical products this way which people would normally pay for, like attractive and interesting jewelry and completed board game sets like self-replicating chess sets. This is a hybrid between viral media, craft production for profit, currency creation, and the generalized philosophical language of Icon Magic.

All of this Icon Magic media creation of course relies on physical machines to make the original prints. This is done with the Trash Robot Geometron printer, made from old DVD drives, plastic trash, cardboard trash, duct tape, Arduino, and some simple off the shelf electronics. All together, these robots cost about 50 dollars in parts, and can be assembled in a day. The skills required are soldering, very basic electronics, and carefully cutting and taping trash into shapes(safe use of a box cutter). We will spread the creation of these robots the same way as all the other parts of the system, where people who know how to build robots share with others. If we can make the products of the robots worth something(both in money and in non-money value) that makes the robots worth something. If the robots have value and area easy to copy, they will replicate. Once we get robots made out of trash replicating freely, we have the basis for building all the other things in our system. This robot architecture can then be evolved into machines that make other machines, machines that make smaller and larger and more complex physical media(like printing books on plastic), agricultural automation, and all the other elements we need to build full Trash Magic and full Geometron as described in other chapters of this work.

Each physically local network hub requires that we build mixed reality media into a public space. This is done with a combination of the physical media here and the digital media of the Magic Books and the infrastructure of the Pibrary. Part of this is building the Map Book of a locality, which means writing text documents and creating maps which integrate stories and knowledge and links into the physical landscape. This only requires that one or two people in any locality really understand our software. The main labor is in the mental process of giving meaning to a space and sharing that meaning. For this we need story tellers, people who are good at connecting people, people who own or control shared spaces, people who spend their days occupying public spaces, and really anyone with an interest in this project to think of types of information they want embedded in a space and to talk with someone who can use the software to integrate all that media into the space. An Operator who knows the system then compiles all these documents in a self-replicating form and replicates them to public facing web pages which are pointed to via the physical media in a physical space.

This system is part of what makes our network financially viable. Building the so-called Map Book or Street Book of a place can link people in a place, and that linking can create enormous economic benefit, which can be kept in the local community and used to materially support our operations. In the simplest sense, this just means we advertise all the local small businesses in a given area and ask them in return to host our infrastructure for free and provide us with resources like free food and a place to work and live.

The aforementioned Operator is someone who learned directly from an existing Operator how to create, edit, delete, and replicate all the documents in our system. We invite you to learn this by asking an existing Operator. You will learn how to create text documents in this system, how to work with our maps, and how all the replication of Cybermagic works. You will learn the ins and outs of the Raspberry Pi, enough to teach other people in the community to learn to use them, and will share them in public spaces with whoever has the greatest need for that resource.

In addition to the Raspberry Pi operators who know

the software and basics of the Pi hardware, we need to train network operators who can build and maintain wireless networks which project free wifi into public spaces. This means learning what to buy and how to install it for wireless point to point links and hotspots, as well as learning the logistics of setting up a dedicated Internet connection in a convenient location which is the source of the network connection. We are not an ISP, and are not selling access. We are simply training people on the level of one small space to create mutual aid based public wireless hot spots.

All of our documents are also always replicated to public-facing web pages on domain names which are connected to physical locations, and we need to ask readers to help build these as well. This means buying a domain and then paying for the monthly hosting costs. In general we assume this will be done by the same people who are maintaining the Raspberry Pi infrastructure, as this is much easier than that, and is just a mirror of that. A domain can cost as little as 10 dollars and hosting can be as little as 10 dollars a month, an insignificant cost for a network which provides any significant value to commerce in a local area.

The Cybermagic code which supports all this also needs developers who can learn how the code works, edit it, and replicate it out to the world using public open source code repositories. As with all other elements of the system, we invite you to contact an existing developer to learn the system and replicate it. The only skills you need to learn this are basic HTML and JavaScript along with a very basic understanding of what PHP does. This can be learned from a combination of an existing Geometron developer and online free resources like w3schools.com and codepen.io.

This network is physical. So we need to physically integrate into a space in order to activate it into the network, and that means we need to travel and stay in places for days or weeks to fully replicate the system. We are also asking readers to invite us, the creators of this network to stay at your home and work in your public spaces to build this. If you can feed and house one of us for a week or two, we can build out all this for free.

In order to build significant hardware infrastructure like long range solar powered wireless Internet links in rural areas, it will be useful to have funding which is not tied to commerce, but is simply there to build things. To this end we need to get grants for network expansion. These grants can come from any kind of sponsor who supports addressing "digital divide" issues. Both physical access to computing/communication resources and the skill set to make use of those resources are one of the forces driving inequality in today's world. Many governments and non profits recognize this issue and have earmarked significant funds to address both of these.

Our system constructs free network access as well as free computers in public spaces targeting the most marginalized(starting with homeless and travelers) and trains the local community to use them. This directly and in a very cost effective way addresses precisely the agendas of these sponsors. Furthermore, each time we replicate the system, we are training people who are then qualified to further apply for grants to support further expansion. Grants we are aiming for are to build things in a specific space. They pay for our time for some period of training and building and also all the hardware. We are aiming for grants in the range of 25-250 thousand dollars over from 2 weeks to a year. Grants will be applied for in collaboration with existing non profits, preferably the public library or university. Grants can be from national governments, tribal governments, large non-profits, or just donations from high net worth individuals or corporations. We are asking readers who are grant writers, workers at a local non-profit, university faculty, librarians or local government people to collaborate to write these grants, and then to pay us, the creators of the network to live in your community and replicate all this. We are also asking readers who fall into the sponsor category as government officials, high net worth individuals, or people at NGOs to help find the right grant recipients to put these collaborations together.

The content of these grants is to buy Raspberry Pis, buy solar power stations, buy wireless network hardware, buy domains, and buy parts for the robots and art supplies, and then to train people in a local community to build physical social media which self-supports in the community. Most grants meant to address the digital divide are not sustainable for communities since they train people to leave to get high paying technology jobs in cities. Since this provides no direct benefit to communities, this means there always needs to be more grant money to sustain the program. We provide a completely different model which is much more cost effective and sustainable, in which the product of our efforts is a *locally controlled* network with deep local knowledge which supports local commerce. This makes the network financially self-sustaining without need for more grants, and keeps the technical skills we teach local, preventing the brain drain that makes a lot of workforce development programs in rural or economically depressed areas self-sabotaging.

For now, the main things we are asking from our readers are what are listed above, which is just spreading the network and the idea of the network. As the scale of our network grows, we are asking for people to create more and more complex new things. We want people to write books! We need you to write all the books we need to build full Trash Magic. If the network is self-supporting, this means you can make a living doing this! Once our network grows, more and more people should be able to quit working for the consumer economy and move to working full time for the network off of the donations and revenue available from those getting benefit from it.

When this becomes viable, we will be supported by the shared desire of the community and can focus entirely on the most important problems for building full Trash Magic. We need you to tell us how to grow food everywhere, how to fabricate all medicines we need, how to build heat engines, harness flowing water, work with the soil to use it and improve on it and live in it, to tell our stories of our shared culture, to create art, and to just form the social matrix that connects all this together.

The bigger we get and the more of these problems we can turn into self-replicating media, the easier all of this will get for all of us. By directing all the benefit initially to the *most* marginalized people in the most public spaces, we grow those spaces and build a new civilization where the baseline of life is comfortable. We want to abolish poverty not by moving everyone into a big house with a nice car but by making the tent cities in public spaces into places of luxury and abundance, with free medicine, free air conditioning, free food, free clean water and sanitation and so on. This is our only path to freedom. We must totally abolish the want of those who have the most want *first*. When we do this, the vast store of human energy which is currently "not working" can form a social network where everyone has value, where just sharing in the community itself is considered a thing of value because it is part of how we replicate our whole civilization.

All of this is much closer than you think! We can do

it. It just starts with spreading this message, it starts with this book, please share it and we can build all this! As you learn things, teach them to others. As you build things, share them. And please help us as you do this by creating media and sharing it, creating videos and other social media posts promoting all these ideas. Every time someone shares all this, the whole network gets more powerful and we get closer to building our new world.

Chapter 13

The Path of Geometron

I am Trash Robot, the author of this book, and this is my plan. I am beginning this self-replicating network of books by replicating my own book as part of a self-replicating set of media. The first step to do this is a book tour. This will be partly virtual and partly physical. If I am touring in a place, I will find a point of contact who can organize local people, and then through them find people to do all the things required to replicate the system.

I am asking people to buy physical books and give them away in public spaces to spread these ideas. If the ideas have the power to make people care about our mission, those people will buy books. If people buy books in any significant numbers, I can support myself as a mendicant, traveling from one community to the next teaching people to copy all the elements of the system. This means in each community we need people to learn to replicate and then keep replicating some part of the whole.

The physical set being replicated here aside from the book includes clay tokens, cardboard signs, laser cut geometric shapes, sewn cloth flags and bags, solar powered Raspberry Pi computers running Geometron, public wifi hotspots, and the printers made out of trash and Arduino which print out the clay media. Also, each set will have either a domain name or a subdomain of some existing domain which will host their local books.

The system will replicate all of the Books of Trash Robot, which include the Trash Magic Manifesto, the first Book of Geometron, and this book, Geometron Magic, as well as prototypes of the local books and any books of Trash Magic which community members choose to work on as the system spreads. We are always looking for new authors to create freely replicating books on the things we need. This includes everything anyone might want to know about building local infrastructure without global supply chains. This includes growing plants and fungi, working with ecosystems, off grid energy, building machine tools, working plastics, circuit fabrication, math, science, philosophy, religion, and really anything we might possibly want to know to build this new society of trash.

But initially on the Trash Robot book tour we will just co-create a map book of a place which activates that place. It is not a news site, nor is it a mere directory. It is a whole *book* about a place, with its geography, history, culture, and commerce, all integrated with a self-replicating set of maps, all linked together. The Map Book is just a format of linked maps and scrolls(text documents). But the Street Book is a whole media set including physical media out in public spaces, maps of the spaces, scrolls linked to maps, public web pages hosting all these documents and physical computing resources maintained by local community members.

Geometron is a mendicant order. That is, we are an order of people who choose to give up building property and money based wealth and to live directly off of the network. This tradition of network building and then living off of the network is one that has been practiced for thousands of years by various religious orders, and we take that as a guide. These orders might initially take a vow of poverty but that is not our intent here and it not needed. Historically, religious orders who started out as mendicants also frequently amassed a great deal of wealth and power, but the basis was always building a social network and then asking for direct voluntary support.

In order for the network to be truly free, we cannot turn this into a business. We instead raise grant money to support our operations and ask for material donations from community members for support of both ourselves and network operations. While much commercial activity can happen *on* our network, the creation, replication and development and maintenance of the network must not be commercial for this to work. We can also make money by selling physical books, but for this to work, again we have to have a total lack of inhibition on replication of digital books, and that means no copyright and no money for book usage.

We write books about places and things and people. We travel and replicate all the parts of the system. Physical media points to web pages which host free books which are mirrors of books developed on free raspberry pi servers and replicated out via Github to the global web pages. We build the Books of the Streets and share them via physical media, which brings in more people to co-create more books. We find writers and teach them to spread their books freely on the Network. We build out a library of books which connect people in local physical areas with each other for the benefit of all.

This is our path, the Path of Geometron. It is a way of existing as creators and keepers of self-replicating knowledge for the benefit of all. We create a knowledge network which provides for those in the most need and creates value for those who already have resources. Those we help will help us, and we will help whoever needs the most help, while also helping as many people as we can always.

We seek to live without property, without money, and without mining. Initially this is impossible. Our whole world is made of disposable mined materials, all land is controlled by the property system, and most resources like food and medicine are held hostage behind pay walls of money.

Every time we incorporate another group of people into our network to whom we provide value we create paths to survive without money.

This is the Path of Geometron, as well as the Path of Trash Magic. We are building a self-replicating network of deep knowledge localized to communities which has the long term intent of building a whole new civilization centered on these local communities and sourcing all material from local trash streams to eliminate all global supply chains and mining completely. If we build these local networks for communities of a hundred to a few thousand people, we can build a few million of them to span the whole world. If we can create a system to build all the media hardware using Geometron fabrication, this system can be the basis of a global information economy without mining which supports all other post-extraction industry.

This path does not require any government or large corporation to make a policy change. It does not require building new empires of central power and control. It only requires that we are able to spread the *desire* to build this system. This is why we call it Geoemtron

Magic and Trash Magic. Because it is the desire we all carry in our hearts for a better world which forms the basis of this network, not any one piece of technology or group of people. We do not need to solve the hard problems. We only need to create the spark which inspires people to choose to try to solve the *right* hard problems. If we can create this spark, we can shake the Universe as we experience it, create a world from sun and trash and the living Earth in which all things are free for all people. Please join us in this project of creation.

We want to replicate. The easiest way to replicate is to attach our replication to existing replication. To that end we must integrate our system into existing replication systems such as religions and other similar spiritual and cultural traditions.

Trash Robot is an art collective. You can be Trash Robot as we are Trash Robot. All this is Public Domain, and is intended to replicate freely. This means that YOU as Trash Robot have just as much a right to sell the physical book as we do. Ask one of us for instructions and we will get you the files you need to publish via the print on demand press lulu.com. No royalties are owed. No one person owns any property, all media is created by the Trash Robot collective and declared as Public Domain with no restrictions of any kind. Anyone who sells keeps all the money. People with more money can buy more copies from anyone who sells them and give them away to anyone else who then has every right to sell them for money on the street. This way as long as books keep getting printed and distributed, money will naturally flow from those who have the most to those who have the least. Books can be sold again and again, they can be used to stimulate cash based mutual aid in our network nodes.

www.trashrobot.org

Go forth and multiply!